GHOST STORIES
of
MICHIGAN

by Dan Asfar

LONE
PINE

Lone Pine Publishing International

©2002 by Lone Pine Publishing International Inc.
First printed in 2002 10 9 8 7 6 5 4 3
Printed in Canada

Distributed by: Lone Pine Publishing International
1808 B Street NW, Suite 140
Auburn, WA 98001
USA

Website: www.lonepinepublishing.com
                www.ghostbook.net

National Library of Canada Cataloguing in Publication Data
Asfar, Dan, 1973–
        Ghost stories of Michigan

        ISBN-13: 978-1-894877-05-3
        ISBN-10: 1-894877-05-5

        1. Ghosts—Michigan. 2. Legends—Michigan. I. Title.
GR580.A83 2002   398.2'0977405   C2002-910213-8

Illustrations: Arlana Anderson-Hale: 99, 102, 211; Arlana Anderson-Hale and Rod Michalchuk: 93, 116, 179
Photos: West Michigan Ghost Hunters Society, 28, 30; Rick Riedel and TravDestRevue.com, 107; Local History Department, Grand Rapids Public Library, 128; University of Pennsylvania Library, Annenberg Rare Book & Manuscript Library, 150; Fred Fleury, 191, 193; Gulliver Historical Society, 205

The stories, folklore and legends in this book are based on the author's research. Sources include individuals whose experiences have led them to believe they have encountered phenomena of some kind or another. The stories are meant to entertain, and neither the publisher nor the author claims these stories represent fact. All website addresses are correct at the time of publication.

PC: P5

Dedication

For all the ghost hunters in the state of Michigan

Contents

Chapter 3: Phantoms in Public

Chapter 4: Haunted Houses

Chapter 5: Specters on the Lakes

Acknowledgments

Truth be known, writing this book was more a journalistic endeavor than anything else, as much of the work has centered on getting the material that would make scary and interesting enough tales. The ends of this pursuit were more fruitful than I could have ever wished, acquainting me with a good number of fascinating people and capable correspondents. This book is as much theirs as it is mine, for as every journalist would surely concede, without quality contacts, there would be no story. I would like to acknowledge those people without whom the completion of this volume would have been impossible.

My thanks to Nicole Bray, whose energy and enthusiasm for the paranormal in western Michigan was invaluable; Lucy Keas, for her genuinely eerie accounts of events in and around Detroit; Jason Cooper, for his thorough treatment of the William Ganong Cemetery; and Brad Mikulka for the straightforward accounts of his society's investigations.

I'm grateful to Dan Campora, for providing me with the details of the Dog Lady in Monroe County; and Sherri McElhaney and Denise Hard, for their accounts of their own experiences with the unknown.

I would also like to acknowledge the quality work of previously published writers who have treated the subject of ghosts in Michigan. The following books inspired and informed more than one story in this volume: Reverend Gerald S. Hunter's *Haunted Michigan* (Lake Claremont Press); Frederick Stonehouse's *Haunted Lakes* and *Haunted Lakes II* (Lake Superior Port Cities Inc.) and Marion Kuclo's *Michigan Haunts and Hauntings* (Thunder Bay Press).

Of course, as any supernatural buff will know, the material in *FATE* magazine, in print now for over half a century, provides a virtually bottomless treasure chest from which to dig, and the June 2001 issue was particularly helpful to me. As well, preeminent paranormal raconteurs Barbara Smith and Jo-Anne Christensen, more than generous with their information, have lent me sources and methods quite helpful in the completion of this book.

There are many others who have contributed their time and expertise: Carl Katafiasz, Susie Fair, Donald F. Darke, Kathleen Marquis, David and Cindy Lott, Joel Kurth, Eric Rasmussen, Ron Jones and Jerry Rolinger.

And I'd like to thank the staff at Ghost House Publishing for putting this book together. Especially my editor, Shelagh Kubish, whose deft skill with the language makes editing look half fun.

Thank you all.

Introduction

You might as well know from the start that I was living under a long-established tradition of skepticism when I undertook writing the work that you now hold in your hands. I am not one given to taking many hops, skips or jumps—let alone leaps—of faith, and usually accept proposed beliefs only when they are accompanied by some sort of evidence or lucid observation. This isn't to say that seeing and believing are consistently and unquestionably intertwined. After all, modern science, with all the wonders it has conceived, affirms that there is an entire universe that exists beyond the realm of our senses. Distant galaxies, cells, molecules, atoms…why not ghosts?

Well, why not ghosts? I found myself pondering the question more than once as I worked through this book. The sheer volume of ghost stories in the state of Michigan alone makes a strong case for consideration. If so many people do believe in the existence of spectral beings and have actually had experiences with ghosts themselves, it would be closer to the foolish side of arrogance to preclude the possibility of ghosts dwelling among us. Never mind that the study of paranormal phenomena is increasingly making inroads into the field of formal science, what of all these people's experiences? At least they should impel us to pause and consider: What if?

And if not, then there's the aspect of social history that lives in a region's ghost stories. While many history books discuss the cause and effect of significant political events of the past, a sense of where the common people were during these momentous episodes is often lost. The folklore of the area brings the people's aspect of their own history back to life. The ghostly legends of the state may give contemporary Michiganders an idea of what trials and traumas their historical counterparts endured in years past, of the love, hate, ambition and jealousy that made them human. Indeed, if nothing else, the folklore puts a human face on the history—lending us a sharper focus on the world past.

Through the ghost stories of Michigan I've acquired a sense of the size of the place, the diversity of its land and people, the depth of its history and the stories of its citizens. I hope you have as much fun with these stories as I did. A suggestion: if the sun hasn't gone down already, wait until it does before you turn the page.

Oh, and if you have ghost stories you'd like to share with me, please write to me care of my publisher, or e-mail me at <info@ghostbook.net>.

Chapter 1

Michigan Ghost Hunters

★ ★ ★

For most of us, the supernatural realm does not figure largely in our day-to-day lives. Ghosts are usually confined to the world of entertainment—in movies and books, around campfires—or set aside for quiet moments when we might muse on the afterlife. Indeed, the material world we live in allows very little room for the immaterial...so much so that many people who have not experienced ghosts firsthand might probably say that they do not even believe in them. There are others among us, however, who, either by natural inclination or the force of circumstance, have become preoccupied with the things that go bump in the night.

Some of these people have set up organizations intended to document, discuss and investigate inexplicable phenomena. Members of these organizations venture off into the night armed with electromagnetic field detectors, digital thermometers, tape recorders and cameras...hoping for any kind of encounter with the nocturnal denizens that most of us would prefer to avoid. These ghost hunters have their own vocabulary, where words such as ectoplasm, Electronic Voice Phenomena, orbs, apparitions, psychokinesis and clairvoyance are bandied about regularly. They investigate haunted houses at the request of homeowners, flesh out any truth that may lie under urban legends and share whatever knowledge they acquire with the public. Most of these organizations do not charge anything to investigate haunted sites; supernatural encounters are reward enough for the few people who are driven by their passion for the paranormal.

The adventures of four of Michigan's most active ghost hunting societies are documented in this chapter. What follows are descriptions of observations of rational subjects on inherently irrational phenomena.

West Michigan Ghost Hunters Society

Nicole Bray, founder of the West Michigan Ghost Hunters Society, was only a child when her worldview widened to include the supernatural. She was just seven years old in the mid-1970s when her father was re-stationed by the National Guard, and her family packed up and moved from Grand Haven to Ionia. While most children would have had trouble enough wrestling with the adjustment to the new environment, young Nicole was contending with other difficulties as well. There was something about the family's new home on Hall Street that didn't feel right. "Right away," Nicole says today, "I suddenly became a kid that was afraid of the dark. Even at seven years old, I just felt like there was something there, there was something in my room; it was like I was always being watched."

It was not that she felt personally threatened by whatever invisible presence was silently staring at her, but the mere fact that there was someone there was enough to frighten her—as it probably would most seven-year-old children. Yet that was not the only problem Nicole had with the house on Hall Street.

"There was a spot outside of the house where the shed connected to the garage, and in that corner…I could never explain it when I was a kid…but I was always terrified of that corner. Even during the day I would walk all the way around the garage just to avoid it. I knew something was there."

She was not the only one. When Nicole was 12, her parents bought a puppy, and the little animal soon developed a vehement dislike for that same spot that Nicole steered clear of. Whenever they would take the pup out into the backyard for some training, the dog would run over to that corner, barking and growling at something that none of them could see. Of course, the puppy's strong reaction to the same area that had petrified Nicole all of her young life did little to ease her anxiety.

Nicole bore her fear in resolute silence. She explains today: "Of course I said nothing to nobody. I grew up with two much older brothers and God forbid if I said something about this to them—the teasing! So I pretty much kept my mouth shut about it."

She began to get more inquisitive about what was happening in the house after her brothers left for the military. "That gave me the freedom to be able to start bringing library books home about ghosts and the supernatural…and try to figure out what this was, what it was that I was feeling, what it was that could be in the corner of that garage."

A year later, Nicole's tingling sixth sense was finally vindicated by her own two eyes. "When I was 13 I fell asleep on the couch downstairs in the living room," Nicole relates. "That was when music videos had first come out, and I had stayed up all night watching *Night Tracks,* a show that started at midnight and played videos 'til the early morning. I remember my oldest brother, George, was on leave from the military and he was home sleeping upstairs. I was lying on the couch at that point when you're not quite awake but you're conscious enough that you can sense sounds around you. All of a sudden I sensed that I wasn't alone in the room."

By now, Nicole was used to this sensation and greeted it more with exasperation than anything else. "My eyes were still closed, and I thought to myself, *Here we go again. You've never seen anything before. There's nothing to be afraid of...just open your eyes.*"

The horrifying sight that greeted her when she finally talked herself into opening her eyes made her blood freeze. "On the other side of the room standing by the window was a man—the apparition of a man. He was kind of bluish white, transparent and there was nothing below his knees where his legs should have been. He was just hovering there staring at me."

Nicole lay staring at the apparition for a few tense moments before snapping herself out of her terrified paralysis. She leapt off the couch and bolted up the stairs to George's room. Barely able to contain herself, she shook her brother awake, bubbling over about the ghost standing in the living room. Of course, by the time the two made their way downstairs the apparition had disappeared. George dismissed the incident; chalking the whole thing up as either a nightmare or the first phases of insanity, he groggily made his way back to bed.

Nicole's family moved out of Ionia when she was 17 years old, and it was not until 6 years after that, when her parents were settled back in Grand Haven, that the topic of the house on Hall Street came up again. "I have no idea how we got on the subject of ghosts. It was something that wasn't much talked about in our family. Anyway, I was at my parents' house and we were all sitting around the table when my father piped up saying, 'Did any of you notice that corner where the shed met the garage? It could be 90 degrees outside...and you could go out against the garage, right there at that corner, and it would be freezing cold.'"

Her mother nodded, admitting that she too had felt the cold spot by the garage, no matter how hot it was outside. Nicole could only stare in disbelief. So she hadn't been the only one that had noticed it! While her parents were able to feel the cold spot by the garage and acknowledged the existence of an entity, she seemed to be the only one aware that the presence roamed the house as well.

"Thank God he never decided to come into the house," Nicole's father said.

"Uh, Dad," Nicole responded over her mashed potatoes, "I think he used to." Nicole told her parents about the apparition that she had seen in the living room when she was 13 years old. And it was then that Nicole gave words to that intangible feeling she had always had of being watched. "That," she explained to her family at the table, "was why I was always so scared of the dark."

There was a long silence. Nicole's father looked at her. "Do you mean to tell me," he finally said, "that your two older brothers who teased you so much, never told you?"

"What do you mean 'never told me'?" Nicole replied, "never told me what?" She stared at her dad, returning his surprised gape.

"Well, we didn't want to tell you because we were afraid that it might scare you," said Nicole's mother.

The tone in her parents' voice was serious; Nicole felt something big was about to happen, "OK, what?" she responded.

It was then, six years after they had moved out of the house that had terrified Nicole through most of her childhood, that her father finally told the story. He spoke with a slow, measured voice. "The former owners, the family that lived in the house before us…the wife took the kids and filed for divorce against the husband. The man understandably got really depressed and one day walked out to his backyard, stood against the garage and committed suicide; he shot himself in the head. In that same cold corner—that's the corner where he did it. That's the corner where he died." The silence around the dinner table seemed to weigh a ton.

For Nicole, it was like a bubble had burst. All of her childhood apprehensions were instantly explained. She says today, "Immediately, it was just like 'click, that's it.' The male apparition I saw when I was 13, that explained the feeling in the house, that's why the corner against the garage scared the daylights out of me. That's when I knew. It all made sense."

Ever since that day, Nicole has been especially fascinated with paranormal activity. It dawned on her that she was imbued with a heightened sensitivity to the supernatural. A few of her friends have been less than thrilled when after a casual visit for dinner or drinks, she has informed them of a strong feeling that their home may be haunted.

It was not until the mid-1990s, however, when the Internet began to grow popular, that Nicole started considering more formal applications for her gift. The numerous websites dedicated to the pursuit of the paranormal introduced Nicole to an entire community that shared her experience and interest in the world of the supernatural. After she discovered the website for the International Ghost Hunters Society, it did not take her long to start scheming on ghost hunting investigations of her own.

On a dark night in October 1999, Nicole and her best friend Vicky went out to the Grand Haven Township

Cemetery to investigate. "Basically, we lasted about 20 minutes," she laughs, remembering the experience. As soon as they got out of their car, Nicole felt that they were being watched by beings that were not living humans. But initially, it wasn't a bad feeling. In fact, Nicole was far from feeling threatened, sensing that the spirits in the cemetery were actually welcoming them. All that changed after they walked down a gravel road from the old part of the cemetery to a newer one. "It was almost like that gravel road was like an invisible barrier," Nicole recalls, "because whoever was around us that welcomed us disappeared the second we went over that gravel road. Walking through the new section of the cemetery, we were feeling absolutely nothing. It was like we were walking through a park. Nothing."

It was when the two decided to walk back down the road to the older part of the cemetery again that they felt a deeply disturbing presence looming over them. "We had taken no more than five or six steps when all of a sudden I got hit with this threatening feeling, like a 'get out now or I'm going to hurt you' type feeling."

Vicky felt the same thing; she looked to her best friend, "Oh my God, are you feeling this?" she gasped in frightened awe.

Nicole's reply was short and to the point: "I think we better leave."

They bolted back to their car, an imminent sense of doom hanging heavy in the air. "The feeling just stayed, it was right behind your neck. It was just there, the entire way to the car."

Reacting purely out of some kind of journalistic instinct, Vicky turned around and took a picture as soon as the unseen presence set upon them. Nicole had gotten some of her composure back after they had reached their car and snapped a picture over the roof of their automobile in the direction that they had just come from. When the photos were developed, Vicky's shot revealed an orb of light behind a nearby tree. Nicole's picture, taken a few minutes later, showed a huge orb hovering right above the car just behind them. Whatever, or whoever, it was, it had followed them the whole way.

So concluded the West Michigan Ghost Hunters Society's first adventure. Joseph Cook, a ghost hunter who had already conducted a few investigations in South Carolina, joined up with Nicole a month after her jaunt into the Grand Haven Cemetery and became an important charter member of the WMGHS. The organization grew during the following years as Nicole's forays into the night became more professional. Today, many investigations later, the WMGHS stands as both an established investigator and conveyor of paranormal phenomena in western Michigan.

The members of Nicole Bray's organization do not charge fees to look at haunted locations and make an effort to publicly document their findings on the Internet. In the interests of educating people about the world of the supernatural, the WMGHS has recently begun posting notices for public ghost hunts in areas reported to be haunted. Anyone who is interested and courageous enough can accompany the experts during these nocturnal jaunts, and given the reports of what happened during their tour of the Nunica Cemetery (page 19), individuals who are expecting strange encounters may not be disappointed. The WMGHS can be contacted on the Internet at <www.geocities.com/wmghost/>.

Nunica Cemetery

Nicole discovered Nunica Cemetery quite by accident, speeding past a graveyard sign that was largely obscured by trees just off Highway 96I. Always on the watch for sites to investigate, the ghost hunter was surprised to find a cemetery she hadn't known about located so close to her base of operations. "Whoa!" she exclaimed as the sign receded behind her, "Did that sign say cemetery?!" It would not be long before she was back to take another look.

Nunica's graveyard is tucked away in the woods of Ottawa County; quiet and secluded, there is very little about the place that might draw motorists to pull off 96I to look around. But for Nicole and the members of her paranormal society, the place may as well be paradise.

It was on a clear day near the end of April 2001 when Nicole found some time to go back to Nunica. She was there by herself, taking what are called "control pictures" of the graveyard, recording the layout of the cemetery so her group might have a solid idea of the way the place was arranged when they returned for their evening investigations. When she got her control pictures developed, Nicole knew that these upcoming excursions into the cemetery would be eventful. "There were orbs, ectoplasmic mists all over the photographs," she says. It was then that she knew she was dealing with a very supernaturally active cemetery.

The graveyard is still used today, with new graves being dug in the new section of the graveyard, but Nicole believes that most of the spiritual activity comes from the old part, which has headstones that go as far back as the 1860s. Many of the dead there were casualties of the Civil War, the Spanish-American War and perhaps a smallpox epidemic that may have claimed the lives of many young—for there is an eerily large number of children buried on the grounds as well. Nicole had also noticed numerous unmarked burial mounds on the site, which could possibly be evidence that the area may once have been an Indian burial ground.

So it appears that there are a number of explanations for the intense paranormal phenomena that members of the WMGHS would soon experience firsthand. In mid-May, Nicole returned to Nunica Cemetery, this time at night and accompanied by two members of the West Michigan Ghost Hunters Society. The threesome immediately felt a strong intangible presence when they got out of their car, but for the first little while at least, it seemed to welcome the mortal interlopers.

Nicole remembers that she stopped and was reloading her camera with a fresh roll of film just before one of the more dramatic events of the evening transpired. "I was loading my camera and just happened to look to the right of me, maybe about 15 feet away, and there was a black silhouette of somebody standing there," Nicole relates, laughing that this apparition decided to appear at the one moment she didn't have any film in her camera. "Just to make sure, I looked over to my left, and there were the two other team members…so it wasn't them. By the time I looked back at the silhouette, it was gone."

After a few more hours of snooping around in the cemetery, the ghost hunters were stopped in their tracks by an entirely different sensation. Whereas before, the trio detected an easy sense of permissiveness from the spirits in the graveyard, things changed in a matter of minutes. "It turned out that the spirits' affability only lasted for a couple of hours," Nicole remembers. "Then we started getting indications that we weren't welcome anymore; it was like we outstayed our welcome."

The air suddenly got very cold, and the WMGHS members were instantly stricken with a heavy sense of foreboding. All three soon felt a single-minded desire to leave. It was then that one of the ghost hunters Nicole had brought along looked down to see that his hands were covered in blood. That was it. Without wasting another moment, the trio headed for their cars and made a hasty exit from Nunica Cemetery.

Things played out pretty much the same when Nicole returned with three members of the WMGHS a few weeks later. At first, the foursome felt welcomed in the cemetery, but a couple of hours into their investigation, the climate got very, very chilly. When the team thought it best that they head back to their truck, the spirits in the cemetery decided to give them some incentive to move their departure along a little bit quicker. "We were walking back towards our pickup when the vehicle started moving," Nicole says. "At first, we assumed that maybe it wasn't put in gear all the way or something. So we just ran up to it, trying to open the door and hop in."

The truck was parked on a tightly curved road that wove through the forest, so the members' efforts to stop the truck from rolling had a degree of urgency: if they couldn't get it started in time, the pickup would roll off the road and into the woods. Unable to catch up with the truck as it rolled down the path, the ghost hunters could only watch in amazement as the truck moved down the winding road. Even though there was no visible being behind the wheel, the vehicle made the right turn to stay on the road and was just about to go into the left turn when one of the members finally got into the pickup and got it started. That concluded the WMGHS's third investigation of Nunica.

Their fourth visit to Nunica took place in mid-June 2001. This time, Nicole posted an announcement on the WMGHS website that it would be a public investigation, open to anyone over 21 who had an interest in the paranormal. Twelve people ended up going on this fourth trip. And it seems that the spirits in Nunica were not shy of all these new faces, for it would be the most eventful evening at the cemetery yet.

The black silhouette that Nicole had seen on her second trip to Nunica reappeared, this time in front of the entire group. "We had split up into two teams, one team of four was on top of a small hill, and the rest of us were on a road some distance away…We were just sitting there waiting for the other team when all of a sudden you could see a black silhouette of somebody walking down the road. We radioed the other team to ask them which one of them was coming down the road."

"Umm, we're all here, and we're watching it too," came the response.

"They were closer than we were," Nicole recalls today, "we could just see that a person was walking down the road, they could make out that it was a female. She walked down the road for about 15 more seconds, turned around over by some bushes and then disappeared. The spot where she

disappeared was where I had seen her that first time."
One of the WMGHS investigators caught this silhouette
on her digital camera; it appeared as an ectoplasmic mist
on the camera's screen.

Another investigator recorded an incident on his own
digital camera later that night. "At one point, there were
about eight of us walking together, when we got this feeling that something was hovering just over us. We decided to
stop and try talking to it, informing whatever it was that we
did not intend to harm it in any way, that it could speak if
it so wished."

The ghost hunters' electrical equipment picked up
a number of strange responses. While they could not hear
anything coming from above, the numerous tape recorders
that were rolling all picked up a high-pitched squealing
noise. One of the investigators, a man named Tom, was
armed with a digital camera and began snapping pictures of
the dark sky above them. "We have those pictures on our
website," Nicole says, "there are orbs right over our heads.
They were right there.

"Also," Nicole continues, "there were a couple of people
who felt like they were being followed throughout the cemetery. When I was told about it, I came to find out that yes,
they were being followed after I took temperature readings of
the air right behind them with a digital thermometer. It was
a warm night, at about 71 °F, but the temperature right
behind them fluctuated between 13 and 20 °F."

Indeed, the cemetery was full of such cold spots that
night. One group was investigating an area that contained
several infant graves when they were hit by a surging cold
force was so intense it "almost hurt".

There was also a new presence intent on making itself known on the night of the public investigation. It quickly became apparent to all that this was the kind of spirit that loved to be the center of attention and perhaps it was drawn out by all the company. "Mr. Bond," as the ghost hunters took to calling the mischievous ghost that never strayed too far from one particular headstone, was an enthusiastic prankster. People coming near his headstone would feel a pair of unseen hands either tugging at their hair or attempting to trip them as they walked. "Mr. Bond" also liked to fidget with the investigators' two-way radios, making them suddenly come to life in a cacophony of static and high-pitched bleeps.

But the most dramatic event of the evening came right at the end of the investigation. Just like the previous visits, there was a general sense of acceptance, even welcome, in the graveyard when the WMGHS began its investigation. But after a few hours, whatever forces were at work in Nunica Cemetery had no qualms about informing the team that their time there was up.

"We made it about three hours," Nicole recalls. "My group was out standing over by the cars; we were all out of film and our camcorders had died so we were just standing there waiting for the other team. They were casually walking, making their way over."

That was just before all hell broke loose. Tom was among the group of ghost hunters walking towards Nicole and her team when the chaos began. "I can't explain it," he would later tell Bray, "it was almost like a door opened up in front of me. Like an invisible door right there out of nowhere."

He had a single picture left in his camera and snapped the one shot that would stand out as one of the most spectacular of any taken during the entire Nunica investigation. When it was developed, Tom's picture showed 30 to 40 orbs hovering in the darkness in front of him.

A moment after the "door" in front of Tom slammed shut, Nicole heard a roar in the distance that seemed to be coming towards the cemetery. "We were all close to the highway, so we were all joking about what sort of truck would make a sound like that, when all of a sudden we got hit by this blast of wind, and this wind was so strong that it felt like we were in the middle of a tornado. We looked up at the sky, 'cause that was our first thought...*where's the tornado?* But it was clear—you could see all the stars. That was when we were struck with that very bad feeling, like we were not wanted there anymore. We looked back at the other team, and they were [running] as fast as they could back to us.

"As soon as they got hit with the wind they got that feeling too. I mean the wind was so incredibly strong, it was hard to stay on your feet; we had to struggle to get the doors open, bracing ourselves against the cars just to stay on our feet."

Nicole was in the same car as Vicky, and they stopped after driving about a quarter mile to rearrange their ghost hunting equipment. A startled gasp escaped from Nicole's mouth when she stepped out of her car, for there wasn't even a trace of a breeze in the air. Just a few minutes' drive from Nunica Cemetery, the night was deadly calm. Nicole intends to send the WMGHS back to Nunica at the first opportunity.

The Ada Witch

At the end of every day, as the sun sinks closer to the horizon, a distinct sense of foreboding fills Findlay Cemetery. Shadows lengthen, the bats come out for their nightly foraging and countless wind chimes, hanging from tree and tombstone alike, are moved by a troubled breeze that wafts through the woods, the air coming to life with plaintive notes ringing through the sylvan dusk. But the chimes, placed there to ward off the leaden presence of discontented spirits, only add an eerie resonance to the oppressive feeling in the graveyard. The sun finally falls beneath the horizon and from out there, somewhere in the woods, the Ada Witch draws nearer.

The town of Ada lies on the Grand River and the mouth of the Thornapple, just east of Grand Rapids. Established in 1857, the picturesque little borough was both a rich farming community and a lumber center during its early days—its first settlers driven by promise of opportunity in the American hinterland. Yet along with the pursuit of material wealth and the dreams of happiness that spurred so many of Ada's homesteaders, a story of morbid human tragedy lies buried in the town's history.

Just over a hundred years ago, a lone pioneer hunter was making his way through the forest around present-day Findlay Cemetery when he stumbled on a sight that instantly threw him into a homicidal fury. There, in a clearing in the woods, he saw his wife with another man. The adulterous exchange was interrupted when the husband charged into the clearing brandishing his hunting knife. Roars of outrage, cries of pain and the sound of struggle rang through the forest for the next sanguinary minute; when silence descended on the glade again, the trio lay in grass that was heavy with their hot blood. The woman was dead, and the wounds suffered by the two men would prove to be fatal about a month later.

Not long after the fight near the graveyard, people began to report strange occurrences in the area. Bluish lights have been seen flitting through the trees on dark nights, sometimes moving with disturbingly precise purpose, following people down the road in the cemetery. Lone hunters have heard the sound of footsteps falling right behind them, only to be confronted by nothing when they turn around to face their stalker. Frazzled by an overwhelming feeling of being watched, these same hunters usually conclude their forays into the forest when a sudden tap on the shoulder sends them into startled convulsions and then out of the woods as fast as their legs can take them.

On other nights, for some reason more ominous and sinister, the events of that horrifying murder seem to play themselves out audibly. People have heard the sounds of a fight from deep in the trees; enraged battle cries, wails of agony and pleas for mercy drift into the nearby tents of alarmed campers. If these outdoor enthusiasts do not leave that night, then they're usually packed up and gone—bleary eyed and terrified—at morning's first light.

And then there are the reports of the Ada Witch herself. The female apparition has been seen both during the day and in the evening, drifting through the woods on weightless legs. Long dark hair flows down her back and her young face is devoid of any expression; she wears a white dress in the style of the late 19th century. No one really knows why

Glowing lights at Findlay Cemetery captured on film.

people have taken to calling her a witch; certainly the ghost has never been seen practicing witchcraft, but it is believed that she is the ghost of that unfaithful woman murdered by her husband so many years ago. It is not known if the woman practiced witchcraft when she was alive.

One of these areas was in a small cluster of several graves set off from the rest of the cemetery by surrounding trees. "When we reached that area, we all caught the horrible odor of decay," Nicole later recalls. "It was so bad that some of the team had to step away for a short while until they got used to the smell. The longer we stayed there, the stronger the feeling got that we were no longer wanted there…that we were making someone very angry." That feeling got so intense that when the team—including a FOX TV cameraman—returned to investigate later in the evening, two team members refused to walk there by themselves.

About halfway through the investigation, the bluish green lights that the cemetery is famous for came out. Everyone there caught glimpses of moving light in their peripheral vision, even the FOX TV cameraman. The problem was that whenever anyone spun around for a direct look, the lights vanished. This ongoing game of peek-a-boo was starting to annoy the WMGHS members, who were frustrated by their inability to capture the lights on film. Joseph Cook, WMGHS founder, came up with the idea of slowing down the shutter speed of his 35mm camera. It worked, and the team came away with a number of outstanding pictures of the green lights at the Findlay Cemetery.

The other area where paranormal activity was especially powerful was in the back of the cemetery bordering the surrounding woods. "The feeling of being not only watched, but surrounded by spirits was intense," Nicole relates. "We were getting between 10- and 20-degree temperature drops around this place." One of the pictures they snapped among the trees near these graves shows an ectoplasmic mist that partially enshrouds the head, face and body of a woman. But the team was only able to take one picture before the mist dissipated into nothingness. Could this have been the Ada Witch? Nicole doesn't think so.

Convinced that everything the team was experiencing was related to spirits from the cemetery and not the legendary love triangle that consumed itself in one fatal confrontation, Nicole took the team away from the graveyard and into the

West Michigan ghost hunter surrounded by ectoplasmic mist at Findlay Cemetery.

surrounding woods where the witch is often sighted. "Unfortunately," Nicole says, "we did not catch any activity."

Lumbering through the forest around Ada with all sorts of recording devices—thermometers, cameras, tape recorders, EMF detectors and film recorders—Nicole's team did not see an elegantly dressed Ada Witch weaving her way through the woods, nor did they hear anything resembling a lethal knife fight. But such are the hazards of ghost hunting; not every night ends with a dramatic supernatural encounter. And given the impressive findings in the cemetery, the WMGHS isn't anywhere near closing the book on the Ada Witch.

The Blue Man

Nicole Bray had known for quite some time that the Forest Hills Cemetery in Grand Haven, Michigan, had an interesting reputation among locals. Not only did the old burial ground have a rich history, with a massive section set aside for those Michiganders killed in the Civil War, but the urban legends of the cemetery's Stairway to Hell had been circulating since she was 18. "Don't go up there," kids had warned her when she moved back to Grand Haven with her family in 1987, "crazy things happen up there."

These warnings were probably kicking around in Nicole's head when she took reporters from a local television station along on a ghost hunt in July 2000. With her small retinue of ghost hunters and reporters, she marched into Forest Hills as night fell on the enormous cemetery. It was then that she looked up at the staircase embedded into the big hill for the first time: the Stairway to Hell. "Let's go up there," Nicole said, pointing to the staircase she remembered hearing about as a teenager, "I want to see what's up there." Indeed, anything with a name like "Stairway to Hell" would be difficult for most ghost hunters to ignore.

But her first climb up the famous stairs ended flatly. They poked around on the hill at the top of the steps for about five minutes without seeing, hearing or feeling a single thing out of the ordinary. So they moved on, intent on going through as much of the cemetery as they could that night. Yet if her experience at the top of the Stairway to Hell was disappointing for Nicole, the popular response to the report she prepared on the place was anything but. Nicole's website was flooded with letters responding to her Internet posting of the WMGHS's investigation of Forest Hills.

Almost everyone who wrote her asked about the Blue Man at the top of the Stairway to Hell. Correspondents young and old grilled her about what she witnessed…had she seen a blue apparition hovering over the tombstone of William M. Ferry? The strong public response to her investigation at Forest Hills provoked her into researching the place. Who was the Blue Man? And why were the stairs that led to him referred to as the Stairway to Hell?

After digging a little bit into the local history, Nicole discovered that the Reverend William Ferry had been a prominent theologian in western Michigan who arrived from Massachusetts in 1834. He was an active and ambitious man of God during his lifetime, setting up a mission on Mackinac Island, starting up the Grand Haven Company, establishing the town of Ferrysburg and co-founding the city of Grand Haven. Given this impressive list of worldly achievements, we may be able to understand William Ferry's reluctance to leave this earth, despite whatever otherworldly paradise he believed was waiting for him.

And as for the moniker, "Stairway to Hell," given to the steps that climb up to his grave, its origins are lost in the folklore of the region, which states that the stairway is a bridge to the afterlife for those buried in the Forest Hills Cemetery. Local legend has it that the souls of the people laid to rest there have to go to the top of the long staircase, where their ultimate destiny awaits. If there is a shining light at the top of the hill, that person will go to heaven; but if the darkness of the surrounding night is all there is to be seen, that soul is doomed to walk back down the stairwell, where the fiery pit of hell lies gaping at the bottom.

As is to be expected, the legend of the Stairway to Hell has resonated with adolescents more than anyone else, and it is teenagers who have had most of the supernatural experiences in Forest Hills. Over the years, succeeding generations of teenagers have gone up the Stairway to Hell with Ouija boards and cameras and have prepared mystical chants with hopes of laying eyes on the Blue Man. Many of these adventurers came to be sorry for what they wished for and walked away from disturbing experiences, claiming that they will never go back up the hill again. Nobody mentions what it is about the Blue Man that's so terrifying.

Her preliminary research on the man completed, Nicole decided it was time to take a closer look at his gravesite. The ghost hunter explains what she saw: "I went up there to take some pictures of the grave—not at night, but during the day, because I was by myself—and I noticed that the two trees right beside his grave had cryptic symbols carved all over them."

Nicole is schooled in basic occult symbology and felt a distinct chill when she recognized that many of the marks on the trees were Satanic symbols. Who carved these symbols around William Ferry's headstone? Did William Ferry make enemies of the wrong people during his lifetime, persons who had the means to exact a revenge that reached beyond the grave? Perhaps the symbols carved into the two surrounding trees have woven some sort of curse on Ferry's soul, binding his essence to his gravesite for eternity. Or maybe Ferry himself did not wish to let go of his earthly being and made some sort of arrangement with Satanists so that a part of his consciousness would live on in perpetuity. The symbols and the origin of the Blue Man are the kind of mystery that the WMGHS is here for, and Nicole's final words on the topic show her matter-of-fact determination: "This is an investigation that's going to be pretty ongoing."

The Michigan Ghost Hunters Society

Though the mainstream rationalism of our age has largely relegated the matter of ghosts to the level of superstition, many of us have lived through experiences so strange that they might make us consider the possibility of paranormal phenomena. Even then, we usually try to find "logical" explanations for whatever bizarre sights and sounds slink through our midnight hours. But what would most of us do if we were presented with a situation that completely precluded any kind of reasonable explanation? Would hard empirical evidence of something that exists beyond the material realm change the way we look at the world? Or would we try to forget such an unnerving encounter and attempt to get on with our day-to-day lives as quickly as we could?

Lucy Keas, founder of The Michigan Ghost Hunters Society (TMGHS), was always conscious that odd things were afoot in her Chicago childhood home. Yet it was not until Easter 1989, when she was 19 years old, that she experienced something that convinced her there was more to the world than meets the eye.

"The folks were away on vacation, and my siblings were at family members' for Easter dinner," Lucy recalls today. "It was about 10 o'clock at night and me and a friend were sitting in the kitchen snacking on junk food."

Their feast was interrupted by a strange sound coming from the back porch, as if something was shuffling about and moving boxes around. Assuming that it was an opossum, raccoon or some other nocturnal critter messing around behind the house, Lucy and her friend stepped out back to investigate. As soon as they opened the door the sound stopped. "No sooner did we sit back down at the kitchen table than the sounds started again," Lucy says. "This time, though, it sounded like the boxes on the back porch were being picked up and dropped."

The loud crashes made the couple jump up from where they sat. Lucy was convinced that someone was trying to break in. In a sense, something was, but it was no human intruder. "The sound of what we thought were boxes falling, those big booms, actually moved through the back wall of the house and into the back bedroom. Something we couldn't see walked right by us, up the creaky wooden stairs and paced the upstairs hallway. It got louder as it went, and by the time it got upstairs, it was so bad that the whole house seemed to shake."

Lucy and her friend dashed out of the house in a panic and ran down the street to Lucy's aunt's place. After listening to their story, the aunt reassured the two teenagers that they could return to Lucy's place and she would send her husband by to take a look. Lucy's aunt did not seem too concerned about the incident, perhaps chalking it up more to teenage imagination than anything else. The two were not back at Lucy's for very long before the thundering footfalls resumed. For the second time that night, they ran terrified from the home, this time not to return until the next day.

Lucy Keas was never the same after that night, when her eyes were irrevocably opened to the spectral world. Not one to ignore something just because it didn't jibe with popular belief, she carried the experience with her for the next 10 years. So she wasn't taken completely off guard when invisible entities came calling again soon after her move to Westland, Michigan, in 1999.

The nocturnal visitors started coming shortly after she had her cat put down. "I could hear my cat's toys being thrown around when I was in bed. Sometimes the blinds would rustle, like a cat was jumping up on the window sill." Such incidents might lead us to believe that the spirit of Lucy's old pet was carrying on in death as it had in life, yet other occurrences suggested there was more at work in Lucy's place than the ghost of her cat.

"One night as I was settling down to sleep," Lucy recalls, "my entire bed shook under the weight of an invisible blow, like somebody big punched my headboard. I heard my name yelled out the same instant that my bed was struck."

And that wasn't all.

"Probably the worst experience I had in that place, the one that made me move out, happened soon after that," Lucy says. "I was living in a duplex suite and my bedroom was on the ground level. My bedroom window was up pretty high, so that if you were a really tall person, you could just peer in; it was my habit to keep this window open at night. Anyway, I was woken one evening with that, by now, familiar feeling that something wasn't right." Lucy's eyes wandered up to her bedroom window, where she saw that the screen on the window was crumpled into a V-shape, like somebody had pushed it in from outside.

"The first thing I thought was that somebody had broken into my house so I called 911. The policemen came by and found no sign of any kind of break-in when they went through my house; nothing was moved, broken or stolen. What's more, when they took a look outside, there were no footprints in the dirt under my window—no evidence that anyone had stood there anytime recently." While police officers were content enough to report that some unknown force pushed in the crumpled screen, Lucy knew in her bones that supernatural forces were at work.

Thinking seriously about the paranormal was no longer a stretch for Lucy Keas. "Somehow, I developed an empathy for spirits; I became much more conscious of supernatural undercurrents wherever I went." After meeting a few individuals who had similar affinities for the supernatural, Lucy became imbued with a desire to know more about the world that existed at the edge of her cognizance.

Juggling her interest in the paranormal with a day job as a telecommunications analyst, she established a website for TMGHS in May 1999, and her investigations in the following years turned her organization into one of the most famous web-based paranormal teams in Michigan. With her consistently dramatic findings, local media coverage and widespread respect among ghost watchers, Keas's TMGHS accumulated over 500 members worldwide and managed to put more than 100 sites on Michigan's cultural map.

Eloise Mental Asylum

The dark shadow of the Eloise Mental Asylum has loomed over Wayne County residents for more than a century. The infamous infirmary was established in 1839, two years after Michigan entered statehood, and until it was closed down in 1981 it was the last stop for those who didn't stick to the American ball of wax. Eloise occupies that dismal space in the public consciousness that teeters somewhere between disgust for the disenfranchised and fear of an alienation that sometimes seems closer than most of us would care to admit. Perhaps this discordant knell that Eloise rings in the minds of Detroiters explains the public furor aroused by Lucy Keas's investigations into the abandoned mental asylum.

It was one of TMGHS's first investigations, and it is safe to say that Lucy had no idea what she was getting into when she let a television crew from a local news channel come along. "If we would have known that the story was going to be that big," Lucy says of the Eloise segment that aired late in 1999, "we would have never done it." The dramatic footage of the ghost hunters in Eloise sent people flocking to the old asylum hoping to catch sight of any ghosts of deceased mental patients. A large number of hopefuls flooded into the structurally unsound hospital, and subsequent issues of public safety, vandalism and property damage impelled the county to hire full-time security. To this day, Lucy feels some personal responsibility for the hysteria that was born around the asylum—a place heavily laden with the ghosts of its tragic history.

Since its inception as the Wayne County Poorhouse in

1839, the Eloise site has been a refuge for those members of society who lived beyond the pale. Originally intended purely as a haven for the poor, by the mid-1040o every sort of problem in Detroit society was being cast out to the poorhouse. Little differentiation was made between inmates who were simply impoverished and others who were judged to be criminals. Those who were deemed insane, however, were isolated on the second floor of a hog barn built on the property. An oft-quoted passage from Stanislas M. Keenan's book, *The History of Eloise*, captures the awful disregard for these people. With poignant brevity, the county employee and part-time historian wrote that the area rang with the sound of "the chained unfortunates roaring and shrieking in discord with the squealing pigs."

Conditions certainly improved for mental patients as a number of medical reforms humanized the psychiatric profession throughout the 19th century; in 1869, inmates were moved out of the pig barn into another building, and by 1881 the mental patients were no longer restrained by heavy metal chains. In 1894, the facility was renamed and divided into two wards: the Eloise Infirmary for the Sick and Elderly and the Eloise Hospital for the Insane. While things improved for the castaways of Wayne County, life at Eloise was no Sunday outing.

The first generations of the 20th century brought another kind of outcast before Eloise's gates. An outbreak of tuberculosis in 1903 saw the number of patients on the compound increase dramatically until the state government and Detroit's municipal council built other facilities where TB patients could languish in isolation from the rest of society. In the 1930s, casualties of the Depression flooded into the halls of Eloise. The number of destitute and mentally disturbed rose to more than 8300. Whether a person was suffering from TB, ruined by economic hardship or afflicted with debilitating illness, no stay at Eloise could be said to be pleasant. For the most part, the hospital just functioned to isolate its patients from society. Little effort was made to cure the inmates, and most of the inmates passed their days staring out windows, studying cracks in the walls or tying and untying their shoelaces.

The 1950s marked the advent of electrotherapy and new levels of overcrowding in what was then called the Wayne County General Hospital. At that time, the institution was one of the biggest psychiatric hospitals in the United States, so when the volts began to fly in mental asylums around the world, thousands of patients convulsed under electrodes in Wayne County. These were the hospital's "boom years," where patients were crammed into packed rooms and beds spilled into the halls. Stories of patient beatings, appalling living conditions and medical malpractice were reported regularly, and the 593 numerically marked graves on the hospital grounds are a testimony to the voiceless suffering so many of the hospital's inmates must have endured. Beset by financial problems and coming under increasing pressure to change by a reforming medical community, Wayne County General closed down in 1981, leaving behind a complex of empty buildings that were to be gradually torn down.

Any history laden with this kind of misery is rich breeding ground for discontented revenants, a fact that Lucy Keas was aware of when she was doing her preliminary research on the place. In the summer of 1999, as she approached the complex on the corner of Michigan Avenue and Merriman Road for the first time, something told her she was on to something big.

"The first couple of times we went in we stayed on the outside grounds, next to the firehouse, one of the only structures that is left standing. During these first investigations, the only thing that really stood out was the smell in the air surrounding the firehouse," Lucy remembers. "It was a sharp, pungent smell, like urine, and it would be thick around the place one moment and gone the next. The strange thing is that on these nights, there was no wind at all, so the odor certainly couldn't have been drifting in on the wind from anywhere else."

Events at Eloise got more dramatic on subsequent outings. "As we got more familiar with the place, we gained admittance into the halls, and it was then that I began to feel the presence of distinct spirits. There was a sense of pain, fear and confusion; sometimes lights would be switched on and off." The group heard "strange growls and moans" coming from another part of the asylum.

One of the most dramatic findings in Eloise came from a tape recorder that Lucy had running when she was looking around outside of the firehouse. Ghost hunters record Electronic Voice Phenomena (EVP) by leaving a digital tape recorder running while they investigate their sites. It's a way to record those frequently occurring noises that members so often are sure they heard when on a hunt. "I was talking about the weather," Lucy says today, "when we all suddenly felt this overwhelming presence and a voice say something like 'sweep you off your feet.' "

It was a charming enough sentiment, so Lucy was at

a loss as to why such a feeling of dread accompanied the sound of the hurried whisper. It was only after they were able to analyze the recording that they realized the voice was saying "sweep you off the earth." The cold chills that the entire team felt that moment outside the firehouse suddenly made sense. Whatever spirit resided there was obviously not happy that TMGHS was stomping around the old asylum.

As for Eloise's graveyard, a large open field with nearly 600 cement plaques imbedded in the ground, there are conflicting reports as to what exactly is going on there. Lucy is adamant that no spirits reside on that burial ground. "I never got any kind of feeling out of the cemetery. It's basically a flat field with numbered plaques marking the burial plots. But nothing, I never got a thing while investigating the graveyard."

Scores of people who came to Eloise in the wake of Lucy's investigation claimed that something sinister hung over the graves. One man who requested anonymity wrote of a very disturbing experience when visiting the cemetery by himself. "I drove out there alone during the day just to get a feel for the place. I got more than I bargained for…There is something at Eloise that was never alive; why it can assert itself there I don't know, but I suspect the area's brutal history has a lot to do with it. When I stopped my car and got out, something told me to leave—something that was once a person. As I approached the cemetery an impression of profound sadness quickly built to a horrible crescendo and then abruptly stopped. The next moment I felt as if I was in a vacuum, being appraised by something that was malevolent."

Lucy Keas dismisses such statements as "teenage melodrama," for after a few local television channels released sensational accounts of TMGHS's forays into Eloise, the old hospital became, to use Lucy's words, "a circus." Human beings are naturally drawn to drama, and after one dramatic depiction of the hospital's history and the ghost hunters' recent investigations on TV, Eloise became a magnet for people in the Detroit area with any kind of interest in the supernatural.

Today, Eloise is known officially—as officially as matters related to ghosts can be—as one of Michigan's haunted sites. The site is on almost every supernatural society's webpage and has been reported on by dozens of nocturnal adventurers. It was TMGHS that put Eloise on the ghost hunters' map. Given all the issues that have arisen because of it, whether Lucy is happy about this or not…that's another question.

The Bath Massacre

Given the nature of their pursuits, ghost hunters may be considered experts not only on the supernatural but also on human tragedy. All too often, the spirits that remain after death wander through those places that have been marked, at one time or another, by the saddest events of a person's life…madness, murder, heartache, loss. It seems that those people subjected to fate's darkest intentions are the ones most likely to leave some part of their essence behind after they've come to their unfortunate end.

So it is that Lucy and TMGHS went from investigating the dark recesses of Eloise to an even more unpleasant place on earth. It was in Bath, Clinton County, where one of Michigan's worst disasters was visited on the local population by the morbid machinations of one man: Andrew Kehoe, the monster who was responsible for detonating over 500 pounds of dynamite under the Bath Consolidated School on May 18, 1927. The ensuing blasts claimed 38 children, 7 teachers and the demented father of the homicidal madness, Kehoe himself. Even now, three-quarters of a century after he himself was ripped apart by the roaring pandemonium he conceived, the man's name is synonymous with evil to residents of Bath.

Essentially, Andrew Kehoe was a man who didn't know how to deal with the world around him. Unable to comprehend the workings of anything outside his own constricted sphere of experience, he was the type of person who couldn't understand why other people didn't see things his way, which was—as far as he was concerned—the only way. Certainly his fervent devotion to such a narrow way of life didn't win him many friends, but many of Bath's influential were impressed by his pragmatism and fierce independence.

In 1926, the citizens of Bath mistook Kehoe's thriftiness, crisp appearance, perfectionism and mechanical expertise for general competence and elected him to the school board. It was probably the most morbidly ironic democratic appointment in Michigan's history.

Kehoe took his seat on the board quite seriously, funneling all his life frustrations into the school policy meetings. It had been a bad year for Andrew Kehoe. His farm was beset by financial difficulties, and his wife was chronically sick with a mysterious illness that no doctors were able to diagnose. Unable to sustain the combined expenses of his wife's medical costs and his farm's mortgage, Kehoe began to perceive himself as a victim of forces beyond his control. For somebody naturally obsessed with governing every smallest detail in his life, this was a hard pill to swallow. He needed some kind of tangible scapegoat for his problems: Kehoe's eyes turned to the Bath Consolidated School.

It was a question of taxes. Kehoe was outraged by the recent developments in the local education system, where the countless rural schoolhouses scattered around Bath were replaced by one large institution in town. Though progressive ideas on education stated that pupils received better schooling in a centralized system, Kehoe couldn't see anything beyond the damage the school was doing to his pocketbook. Building and sustaining the new school meant increasing taxes, a burden that the financially strapped farmer could not carry.

As his fiscal situation grew worse, Kehoe began to view Bath Consolidated School as the source of all his problems. Obsessive, self-centered and completely paranoid, Kehoe's myopic view of things went from bad to worse, and he was soon scheming up a way to lash out at a world that was obviously out to get him.

In the winter of 1926, the school board hired Kehoe to be the maintenance man for Bath Consolidated School. Now that he was given easy access to the school grounds, a plan of vengeance started to crystallize in the man's head. He began to take regular trips to Lansing, purchasing small quantities of dynamite from a local sporting goods store. A few months later, in the spring of 1927, Andrew Kehoe had stockpiled over a ton of explosives at his house.

He spent most of the last few months of his life painstakingly preparing for the diabolical project that possessed him, sneaking wiring, charges and explosives into the school during the early spring months. By May Kehoe had enshrouded the entire school in a web of imminent destruction. Wires linked by an intricate system of detonators snaked through walls and wound around hidden rafters and pipes. Over one ton of dynamite was divided and hidden in different locations wherever there was room enough to store it. Everything was in place by the time the second week of May rolled around; Kehoe was ready to make his perverted mark on the world.

The first bomb that rocked the town of Bath on May 18 came from Andrew Kehoe's farmhouse. The place was engulfed in flames when Kehoe's neighbors got close enough to see the man tearing towards the school in his pickup truck. A few minutes later, an enormous explosion ripped through the Bath school. Dozens of rescue workers were digging through the rubble of the building when Kehoe arrived at the site in his truck. The day before, he had loaded explosives and metal junk in the back, turning the vehicle into a homemade bomb. He detonated his truck seconds after he drove up to the school, and a fiery ball of shrapnel rolled over the assembled workers. Kehoe was killed along with those claimed by this last explosion.

The horrific day, saturated with the death of innocents, would be burned forever into Bath's consciousness. When the firemen went to Kehoe's house to put out the blaze, they found his wife's body lying limply in a wheelbarrow in his backyard, her head having been smashed in with a blunt object. His only message to the public was painted on a wood placard wired to his fence; it read "CRIMINALS ARE MADE, NOT BORN."

The blood-soaked madness of that morning guaranteed that Andrew Kehoe successfully disgraced his way to the upper echelon of the criminal population, but it could have been much worse. It turned out that only about half the explosives that Kehoe planted actually went off. Another 500 pounds set to explode about 45 minutes after the initial explosion never detonated, and police surmised that the wiring was probably damaged by the first blast. Of course this was scant comfort to the friends and family of the 45 people who were killed—38 of that number being children.

Lucy Keas stumbled on this tragedy while researching Michigan's history, and her gut told her she was in for an interesting investigation the moment she read about the 1927 massacre. She wouldn't be disappointed; all of her forays to the Bath memorial site have resulted in dramatic findings.

Lucy was by herself the first night she visited the memorial park, and though nothing out of the ordinary happened through most of her visit, she was aware of an extreme sense of sadness hanging over the place. "I was getting nothing all night. No pictures, no recordings," Lucy remembers. "In one part of the field where I got an especially strong feeling, I asked whatever was there if I could take a picture. There was no response."

Certain that the place was haunted by Kehoe's victims, Lucy resigned herself to the fact that no children were going to reveal themselves that night and turned to leave. "I was saying goodbye to the children, promising them that I'd be back, when all of a sudden I heard this chorus of children's voices cry, 'Please don't go, please don't go, we'll let you take our picture.'" Lucy spun around and snapped a shot with her digital camera. The image she captured revealed about 20 orbs of light in the darkness.

On her second trip to Bath, Lucy brought a few TMGHS members with her, intent on capturing more evidence of haunting. A number of bizarre events certainly did occur, but the plaintive voices of sad children that Lucy experienced on her first excursion were replaced by activities that were not nearly as accommodating. Lucy recalls: "All the levers of our cameras would repeatedly pop open by themselves and the batteries would spill out. At one point, I was standing there in the middle of the field talking to one of my members when I was overcome with this feeling of fear and sadness. All of a sudden I burst into tears, for no real reason at all."

Paranormal activity increased on subsequent visits, and Lucy would become aware of a disturbing presence that haunted the park. The first time she observed this being was during her third trip, when she saw the shimmering figure of a man running around a cupola that had been preserved from Bath's first school. No one else saw the apparition. The man appeared again about an hour later, at which point Lucy approached the cupola; she was suddenly overcome with anxiety. "What do you want from me?" she said aloud when she got there. "Why are you running around the bell tower?"

A member of TMGHS was close by Lucy with a tape recorder running; she captured the figure's response to Lucy's questions on tape: "Don't come back here, get out, get out…thank you."

The last time TMGHS went out to Bath was the most dramatic visit by far. Lucy was out walking in the middle of the field, quite close to the fenced-in cupola when she felt the presence of what she knew then was Andrew Kehoe himself. "I was having 'words,' so to speak, with this…murderer," Lucy recalls with nothing but contempt in her voice when she refers to Kehoe. The psychic exchange wasn't really verbal, but rather more like an unspoken exchange of feelings. Lucy was struck by a strong impression that Kehoe was taunting her, laughing at her nocturnal jaunts to Bath, telling her that she was "wasting her time." Seconds after Lucy communicated to Kehoe that she wasn't afraid, she was struck by a sudden wave of nausea. It was so bad that she had to leave the grounds for a time.

Returning to the park later that evening, Lucy recalls that it was not long before the ghost of Kehoe focused on her again. "I was standing right next to the bell tower, tinkering with my camera, when I felt something like warm water trickle down my leg. I looked down and saw a wet spot in the middle of my calf. It literally felt like something had peed on me. I instantly got a few of the other members over and told them what had just happened. When I said that it felt like something peed on me, this kind of snickering came out of nowhere, and a voice said 'good boy!' like a man would if he were talking to a dog." This too, was captured on tape by a member of TMGHS.

This was TMGHS's most recent trip to Bath, but definitely not their last. "He's a very active spirit," Lucy says of the detested ghost she has had more than one run-in with. Something about the tone of her voice says that she will go back to Bath before too long.

House Possessed in Livonia

From time to time, Lucy Keas has been called on by people of metro Detroit to take a look at homes they suspect might be haunted. Though Lucy does not maintain that she's able to rid any abode of undesirable spirits, she has been able to tell distressed homeowners what to do when they are faced with situations beyond their experience. Yet these investigations have not been all about the supernatural; indeed, Lucy has learned as much about human nature as she has about the paranormal while investigating other people's homes. When actual ghosts have been lacking, hoaxes, cons and neurotics have abounded, and Lucy has spent more than her fair share of time investigating the motives of beings that still reside on this side of the grave. She was in for quite a surprise, however, when she answered a call from a family living in Livonia, a suburb on the western outskirts of Detroit.

"It was an experience that no one would believe unless they were there," Lucy says today, a trace of awe in her voice as she recollects her experiences in the house.

True to her policy of maintaining homeowners' anonymity when she conducts private investigations, Lucy discloses neither the building's street address nor the residents' names when she speaks of the house in Livonia. Given what transpired in the place during Lucy's three visits, the owners are probably quite grateful for her integrity. "What we thought was an extremely active poltergeist," Lucy says of the incidents in Livonia today, "turned out to be something much, much worse."

TMGHS members visited the home three times during their one-week investigation in March 2001, at which time they observed what Lucy calls "the crème de la crème" of her supernatural experiences. "I was contacted by the owner," Lucy says, "because she really didn't know what to do anymore; she was on her last straw." Lucy and her team found out exactly why after spending their first night at the house. "We were there from nine o'clock at night to five o'clock in the morning on our first night. What I saw there on that night made every other poltergeist activity I'd ever witnessed before look like nothing."

The ruin visited on the house suggested the presence of a very strong and very angry poltergeist. "It was absolutely unbelievable," Lucy recalls, "throughout the entire night, I made sure that we kept up a controlled environment. The two parents and son that lived in the house were always in plain sight. I wanted to keep the variables down to a minimum so there would be no question as to who was touching what."

Her efforts at controlling the environment ensured that the noises coming from the other rooms in the house were not a result of any human hijinks. But then again, whenever the group would run into whatever room the racket was coming from, the sight that greeted them could not have been produced by human hands. "When I say that these rooms were trashed," Lucy says today, "I'm putting it mildly."

According to the ghost hunter, every single item in each room would be "taken down, moved, flipped over, hid in the refrigerator or jammed under the carpet" at some time during the night. "Things would be rearranged in ways that were physically impossible to balance," Lucy recalls, such as glasses "perched on top of forks which were standing on end."

Kitchenware and utensils would somehow disappear "and then rematerialize somewhere else," and the television, originally in the living room, "would somehow relocate to the top of someone's bed. Light bulbs screwed into sockets were heaped into the toilet, and unplugged house appliances would suddenly come to life." One room at a time, the house was reduced to shambles.

If this wasn't unnerving enough, the group in the house would hear whistling coming from the other rooms, beckoning Lucy and her entourage to witness the new destruction. "They made this noise, it sounded like they were calling dogs with a whistle. Every time, they knew we would come running to see what they had done."

Lucy now refers to the supernatural perpetrators of the destruction as "they," but she did not always assume that she was dealing with more than one spirit. Initially, Lucy was led to believe that a small family that had previously lived in the home had experienced some kind of tragedy, and that the presence of the new family—mother, father and son—spurred on the memory of some extreme emotional trauma suffered by the first family. This tidy enough theory did not hold. While Lucy could not find evidence of any dramatic history, events in the house suggested that they were dealing with something far more sinister than she had originally surmised.

"The difference between poltergeists and regular spirits boils down to a higher level of consciousness. Poltergeists are conscious, interactive spirits," Lucy explains, "they're usually attracted to people rather than places, and they'll play you like a game of chess." Lucy pauses briefly, making sure she chooses her next words carefully. "Demons, on the other hand, represent a much graver mental and physical threat than poltergeists. Their one purpose is to drive you out of your mind, so that they can take over."

There was more than one hint that the small family in Livonia was dealing with forces of a Biblical bent. For one, there was the spirits' predilection for one passage in the gospel. "There was one room with a Bible in it, and whenever that room was trashed, the Bible would be open to the same page. It was in the Book of Isaiah, Chapter 47, Verse 3." The passage reads: "Revealed is thy nakedness, yea, seen is thy reproach, Vengeance I take, and I meet not a man."

As the night progressed, Lucy managed to get some additional information from the family members. She discovered that they had had similar experiences in their previous home, though the events there were not as dramatic as those in their current house. The parents told Lucy that they believed "something their son had done" brought on the vengeful spirits. To protect her clients, Lucy has withheld what, exactly, that "something" was. Furthermore, the family told Lucy that they had called a priest before they spoke to her, and that a man of the cloth came in to bless the place a few days previous. The activity had actually gotten worse since the priest had visited.

By five o'clock that morning, Lucy had determined that it wasn't ghosts, but demons, which were wreaking havoc in the Livonia home. "It was time for us to go, so I requested a reprieve for the family, asking the forces there to let the house be for at least 24 hours." The family was granted the time, but when the disturbances began again, they were worse than ever.

Lucy visited the house for the second time a few days later. She was shocked at the sight that greeted her when she got there. It seemed that the parents at the home invited everybody they knew to witness the investigation that night. "It was a complete circus," the ghost hunter recalls, "none of their friends and family believed what was happening, and they all wanted to be there to see it for themselves." Of course that would be the night when the family's tormentors decided to lay low. "We really didn't get anything done. We couldn't—there were just too many people there." All Lucy detected that night were traces of "different smells," but nothing happened that came close to the bedlam during their first night at the place. The investigation turned into more of a social call than anything else, where Lucy found herself conversing with a room full of people who were content with meeting a ghost hunter even if they couldn't witness any real-life ghosts.

But things quickly got worse for the family after all their guests left. By the time Lucy dropped in for her third visit two nights later, the household was desperate. "That was the night I told them they should call in another priest," Lucy says. But even as the clergyman was walking through the house reciting prayers, the unholy activities continued. It was then that Lucy determined a formal exorcism would be the only solution to the problem.

The next day, a priest from another church paid the family a visit to perform the lengthy ritual of exorcism. Lucy spoke to the woman of the house two weeks after the exorcism was done. "She claimed that the house was very quiet," Lucy says. After that, TMGHS never heard from the family again—with the exception of the son, that is.

"The son actually tried to call me once, about three weeks after," Lucy remembers. "I knew something was wrong, but when I called him back, I never got a response. So I asked the daughter of a friend of mine, a girl who went to school with the boy, to talk to him for me, to tell him that I was here for him if he wanted to talk. Apparently, he didn't react well when my friend's daughter approached him. He told her that he didn't know what she was talking about, and that he didn't want to speak to her again. So whatever actually ended up happening in that house, I'll never know."

Members of TMGHS have had plenty of time to mull over what was going on with that family. Lucy's group came up with a theory that countered the parents' assertion that it was something their son had done. Yet whatever that theory is will remain locked in TMGHS's vaults, protected for purposes of client confidentiality. "We know what the incidents stemmed from," Lucy says, "and it did not happen because of the son. One of the other adults was responsible—that's all I'm willing to say."

Michigan Organization of Paranormal Activity Research

Jason Cooper's fascination with the dead goes back to his childhood years, to the day that his young eyes spotted the name "Hannah Pennibone" on the massive granite gravestone hidden in his grandfather's basement. A trophy from a night of youthful mischief, the displaced headstone was pulled out of the ground in an abandoned cemetery in Ypsilanti and dragged into the house by six teenagers. It was Cooper's adolescent uncle and five friends who snuck into the Highlands Cemetery late in the night and emerged from the darkness a few hours later with the 500-pound monument to the long-deceased Ms. Pennibone.

Where does one put a stolen headstone? Uncertain of what to do with the grave marker, and probably deterred by its size, the Cooper family just left it alone, and the ornate tombstone became the household let's-take-care-of-it-tomorrow project. As for young Jason Cooper, the sight of the huge block of stone looming in the shadows of his grandfather's basement struck a chord in the boy. The future founder of MOPAR spent many an hour gazing at it, running his fingers along the grooved letters of Hannah Pennibone's name, silently absorbing the implications of the distant date, 1880, chiseled just under the woman's name. The granite block and the dark mystery it represented would occupy a large part of Jason Cooper's psyche.

The Highlands Cemetery was declared a historical site in 1997, and Jason answered the newspaper advertisement asking for missing headstones by returning Ms. Pennibone's.

It would be another two years, in the summer of 1999, when Cooper would act on the lifelong interest that the gravestone had instilled in him. For late in August of that year Jason combined his affinity for web design with his passion for the supernatural and set up the webpage for his newly formed institution, the Michigan Organization of Paranormal Activity Research (MOPAR). The website address is <http://www.envy.nu/mopar/>.

Recently, operational difficulties have limited MOPAR's investigations, but Jason Cooper is determined to continue the society's ghost hunts as soon as he is able. The vast majority of MOPAR's nocturnal forays take place outdoors, almost exclusively investigating cemeteries. Of all its supernatural surveys, Cooper's organization has covered the William Butler Ganong Cemetery most thoroughly.

Ganong Cemetery

William Ganong Cemetery is one of Michigan's most famous haunted places. Near the top of almost every ghost enthusiast's list of haunted sites, the cemetery rose to paranormal prominence soon after the late ghost expert Marion Kuclo included a discussion of the old burial ground in her book, *Michigan: Haunts and Hauntings*. The long-since inactive graveyard, which dates back to the 1830s, lies on Henry Ruff Road in Westland and is named after one William Butler Ganong, one of the area's early farmers. Souls resting there seem to have laid low through most of the cemetery's history, not causing much commotion until fairly recently, when stories of strange goings on began to circulate in the late 1970s.

It has been suggested that renovations in the cemetery resulted in a number of gravesites being disturbed—and that the souls of these exhumed graves are currently haunting Ganong. There was also an incident some 20 years ago when heavy rains unearthed a female skeleton still wearing a remarkably preserved white dress. Ever since, a shimmering apparition of a woman in white has been one of the most common sites appearing before spooked witnesses …many of them passing by the cemetery in cars. And of all the bizarre images that have suddenly appeared in the headlights of motorists driving by Ganong, it is the woman in white who has been responsible for most of the car accidents that have taken place on the infamous stretch of road known as the "Bad Curve."

Jason Cooper had become aware of Ganong Cemetery while surfing the Internet from his home in Ypsilanti in

August 1999. The seed that was planted in his mind all those years ago in his grandfather's basement was about to floresce into an active interest in the supernatural. Tired of dwelling on the innumerable accounts of what was happening in a Westland cemetery just a few miles east of his hometown, he finally decided to go take a gander for himself.

He was accompanied by a handful of friends during his first nocturnal jaunt among Ganong's gravestones…unaware that on that hot August night, he and his friends were embarking on the first of many MOPAR investigations in the famous cemetery. The group that went out on the first night was not expecting much to happen, and if the backdrop of an old graveyard at night provided an eerie enough setting, it still didn't make the explorers believe in the supernatural. "Most of my friends that were out with me that night weren't taking the whole thing too seriously," Jason recalls, "they were horsing around, making noise, hamming it up for the camera and what not."

But their sarcastic skepticism was erased when they got back to Jason's home later that night. Cooper had kept a video camera running during the entire investigation, and the moment he plugged the videotape into his VCR, there was only an awestruck hush as disbelieving eyes gaped at the incredible images on the screen before them. Somehow, the camera had captured things that their naked sight had not. Orbs and apparitions abounded in those same places where they had seen only darkness a few hours before.

"At one point, when we were standing in the oldest part of the cemetery, the camera recorded five orange orbs soaring up from a headstone and arcing through the air towards us," Jason says. Even now, two years after the event, there is still a trace of wonder in his voice. "We couldn't see anything when we were at the cemetery, but there they were on the TV, these five lights."

Orbs were not the only eerie images that Cooper captured on his video camera. "The first thing that I did when we got to the cemetery was pan my camera across the grounds from the outside of the fence. On the tape, you can actually see a figure with a whitish head and hands and a dark trunk lying there on the other side of the fence. It sits straight up and looks straight towards us when the camera moves over it. Of course I didn't see this thing when I was filming, so I kept moving past the figure. Two more shadow figures appear in front of me."

MOPAR was born from these spectacular findings, and 6 of the 10 or so people who went out to the cemetery became members of Cooper's organization. "The results of that first investigation got us really interested and fired up to buy more equipment and keep going out," Jason says. Further events during the next few forays would cement William Ganong Cemetery as the organization's principal destination.

The freakish apparitions that appeared on camera during the first outing to Ganong seemed to have acquired voices by the time MOPAR returned two days later. "On that night, we actually heard some screams from the woods. Strange sounding screams—distant sounding—like they were echoing from a tunnel. Everybody heard them, and they're also recorded on our video cameras. A girl screams three times, followed by a plea for help. On the tape, you can hear a desperate 'Help me!' coming from the trees."

Jason and his friends had a strong feeling that the voice they heard was not a human one, but were not so certain that they did not search through the surrounding woods just in case something bad truly was happening. They found nothing there.

MOPAR visited Ganong Cemetery a number of times over the following year, consistently observing dramatic supernatural phenomena during each outing. But it was the fifth excursion into Ganong, on the night of September 30, 2000, that stands out in Cooper's mind as the most bizarre.

"The orbs that we caught on camera were different than before in that they were coming really close, and though we couldn't see them when we were taping, we could actually feel them flying by: it was like you'd suddenly get really cold and your hair would stand on end. When we got home and watched the tapes, we saw that the orbs were moving so close that they actually made a whistling sound as they sped by—a 'whooshing' sound that you can actually hear on the tape."

One of the MOPAR members had such a harrowing experience with the orbs that night that he ended up relinquishing his membership with the organization. It began when the ghost hunters heard the sound of massive movement in the woods. The enterprising MOPAR member climbed on top of one of the headstones to get a better shot of what was going on in the area; what he captured atop the tombstone would go down as MOPAR's most spectacular supernatural footage. "He got countless orbs flying from the gravesite up over the surrounding woods. One of the orbs hit a tree branch as it was going up, and on tape, you can see the bough physically shake and leaves fall under the impact."

His recording was dramatically interrupted when what was apparently another orb actually collided with him. "When he panned to the left," Jason explains, "an orb flew directly up and hit the camera, making it shake. On TV, the collision sounds something like a small explosion and the camera is jolted violently. We have that footage on our website."

When the ghost hunters watched the footage later on that night, the man who had recorded it decided he had enough. "I'm done with this," he said to Jason, "it's too much, they're actually touching me...I just can't handle that." It was almost a year before curiosity overcame fear and the man was once more back with MOPAR.

In a sense, William Ganong Cemetery is the paranormal property of ghost hunters all across Michigan, and almost everyone in Michigan who is interested in the supernatural is aware of the place. The old cemetery in Westland is one of the popular paranormal pilgrimage destinations, and accounts of hauntings there have been reported by more than one ghost hunting organization and journalist. But of all these organizations, MOPAR has done the most work on the site, concentrating almost exclusively on the cemetery for stretches of time. Indeed, William Ganong Cemetery has almost become MOPAR's pet project—an ongoing investigation that continues today.

Southeast Michigan Ghost Hunters Society

For as far back as he can remember, Brad Mikulka has been fascinated with spectral matters. He did not witness any ghostly apparitions drifting through his childhood years; he does not boast of a heightened sixth sense; nor was there ever one defining moment in his life when he knew that he was destined to immerse himself in the spirit world. Brad's mother does claim that the family lived in a haunted house when he was two years old, but if the fledgling ghost hunter had any bizarre experiences at that age, they are buried deep in his subconscious, as he claims there was nothing especially extraordinary about his childhood.

Nevertheless, Brad Mikulka is one of the most enthusiastic paranormal investigators in Michigan today and is the second president of the Southeast Michigan Ghost Hunters Society (SEMGHS). The society, founded in 1998, is one of the original paranormal organizations in the state. SEMGHS exists to provide a meeting ground for ghost devotees in Detroit and the surrounding area, educate individuals who have questions about the supernatural and also assist people who may be having difficulties with spirits in their homes. The SEMGHS does not charge anything for their services.

Brad Mikulka only laughs when he is asked if he has any psychic abilities. "I wish I did," he replies, "but no, I've got no gifts like that. A few of our active members do have heightened sensitivity to spirits, but most of our investigations rely more on scientific indicators of supernatural phenomena."

Scientific indicators of supernatural events? While such a statement might sound strange to the average reader, ghost hunters make use of a number of different instruments that provide quantitative evidence of paranormal activity. "EMF meters, which register changes in the electromagnetic field, also indicate the presence of spirits," Brad explains. As mentioned in the account of the WMGHS's investigation of the Nunica Cemetery (page 19), digital thermometers are another standard tool in the ghost hunter's arsenal. A sudden drop of temperature is the most widely acknowledged sign that there is a ghost in the immediate vicinity. Though Mikulka cannot say that he has ever had any psychic connection with ghostly beings, his society has collected substantial evidence that things exist beyond our senses. According to the ghost hunter, objects that seem to escape our eyes and ears are often captured by digital cameras, tape recorders and video cameras. "From what we have gotten so far from film and video footage," Brad says firmly, "there is no doubt in my mind that there's something out there."

He's not the only one who believes this. Ninety percent of the SEMGHS's investigations are in private residences, and the society is so busy that it is booked two months in advance. Mikulka feels a certain responsibility when he takes a look at clients' homes. "When people contact us, they usually need our help. They might have a situation that they can't take anymore; they may have just moved into an old house and have been experiencing all kinds of trouble—whatever it is, we do everything we can to educate them about what is going on. We analyze footage of the investigation, we have psychics go over the place with us and then get back to the residents of the home as quickly as we can, usually within 30 days. Often, these people aren't so much frightened of the ghosts themselves, but are just looking for some peace of mind—somebody to tell them that they aren't going crazy."

Mikulka ceased being surprised by the sheer number of hauntings in Michigan long ago. "Ghosts are everywhere," the SEMGH's president asserts, "there doesn't have to be a traumatic history for there to be a ghost in the area." Brad's belief that our world is populated by spirits that exist just beyond our ability to sense them means that he doesn't think it's necessary to delve into a place's history to find an explanation for a haunting. On the same note, such a belief demands a greater vigilance from ghost hunters, as it implies that there are many more ghosts on the earth than is commonly believed. With spirits potentially lurking behind every corner, a ghost hunter must always be ready for a supernatural encounter. To read accounts and see pictures of more such encounters, access the SEMGHS webpage at <http://www.semghs.org>.

Cemetery Near Maple Rapids

Brad Mikulka was visiting his mother in Gratiot County in October 1998 when he discovered a small cemetery about a mile or so northwest of Maple Rapids. He was especially drawn by the sight of a small mausoleum on the cemetery grounds and decided to punctuate his visit with a little ghost hunt. "I just had a feeling about that mausoleum," Brad recalls, "I really wanted to look into it."

Mikulka had no personal connection to the family entombed in the mausoleum, nor was he aware of any exceptional history in the graveyard. Nonetheless, if ghosts are everywhere, as Mikulka believes, the population density of revenants in a tomb must certainly be higher than most other places. The ever-vigilant ghost hunter's hunch about the mausoleum was right.

Standing before the mausoleum doors, Brad Mikulka took a couple of deep breaths, steeled his courage and walked down into the tomb, closing both the doors behind him. Alone in the utter darkness of the burial chamber, Brad was suddenly stricken by the oppressive silence of eternity. The 20-some people entombed in the mausoleum may have made a lively bunch when they drew breath; the stillness of their gathering in the ever-after, however, was more poignant than any word they could have uttered when they were alive. Brad stood, frozen in place for countless moments before he gathered up enough nerve to step forward. So heavy was the silence the sound of his footfalls broke that he may as well have had cymbals attached to the soles of his shoes.

"I walked all the way down to the end of the aisle and stopped, taking EMF readings and talking aloud the entire time. I was asking if there were any spirits in the room that wanted their picture taken, [saying] that I wasn't there to hurt anybody, that I only wanted to help." Brad walked up the aisle and back again before he stopped. He shook in startled surprise as the sound of three more footsteps sounded right behind him. Spinning around in a moment of fear, he was greeted by an inky blackness. Brad raised his camera and took a picture of the dark hall in front of him.

Just to make sure that he wasn't hearing things, Mikulka repeated his walk up and down the hall; this time there were no extra footsteps. Later on, when Brad took a look at the picture he had snapped in the mausoleum, he was not surprised to see a single orb of light in the darkness. The presence that escaped his eyes was captured as a circle of light through the lens of his camera. This photograph is posted on SEMGHS's website.

The next time that the SEMGHS returned to the cemetery near Maple Rapids in April 1999, the mausoleum doors were locked, so Brad went ahead and investigated the rest of the grounds for spirits. Brad's theory about the ubiquity of ghosts was again validated by traces of another presence that hung over a Feetham family tombstone. SEMGHS members figured out something wasn't right about the tombstone when they recorded temperature readings around the gravesite that were several degrees lower than the general temperature. They snapped a series of photographs, all of which revealed a thick ectoplasmic mist hanging over that one headstone. Ectoplasm, residual matter produced by ghosts, is another supernatural substance that is usually invisible to the naked eye but shows up on video footage and in photographs. The SEMGHS hasn't visited the cemetery by Maple Rapids since, yet Brad is certain that they will find more ghosts when they go back to investigate.

Historical Graveyard in Mason

It was mid-August 2001, and Brad was on a guided tour through Mason's oldest cemetery. It was a pleasure trip for the ghost hunter; he surely wasn't looking for ghosts on the bright, sunny afternoon when he was the recipient of a slap in the head. "The guides giving the tour were talking about the historical significance of one specific tombstone when something hit me upside the head. It was broad daylight and I assumed that somebody on the tour was trying to start something. But when I turned around there was nobody there."

Brad's wife, Brenda, was with him on the tour of the cemetery and saw him react when he got hit. "What?" the alarmed woman asked her husband.

"Something just hit me!" Brad exclaimed.

Mikulka couldn't deny that something otherworldly was trying to get his attention, and so it was that an innocent weekend outing turned into another ghost hunt. "I began taking a lot of pictures of the tombstones and sure enough, the photos were riddled with orbs of light." One building near the front of the cemetery served as a repository for coffins that were about to be buried. When Brad snapped a picture of that structure, he got five orbs hovering around it. Again, what Brad, Brenda or anybody else on the tour couldn't see with their own eyes in broad daylight was captured by the camera's lens. Thus investigating the cemetery in Mason has been added to the SEMGHS's "to do" list.

Known by all ghost hunters simply as "orbs," the circular spots of light, varying in size and brilliance, that appear in photographs are the most popular indicators of supernatural activity. The rule is that where there are orbs, there are ghosts, and the webpages of most ghost hunting societies are full of photographs spotted with these inexplicable circles. If these circles actually do represent supernatural energies, as ghost hunters are wont to believe, then the world truly is populated by unseen hosts of spiritual entities. A large number of the SEMGHS's findings around Michigan are available on the society's webpage.

The Linden Hotel

What once was a hotel in the small town of Linden now houses a family restaurant on the ground floor and a sports bar upstairs. One of the town's older buildings, the Linden Hotel was built in the 19th century and long served as the town's premier stopping point for people in temporary need of roof and bed. Renovations and subsequent proprietors changed the nature of the business in the building, but just as is the case in many old houses, it seems that things that came before sometimes have a way of sticking around. Indeed, if the ghosts in the Linden Hotel could speak, the voices drifting through the building's halls might whisper of the power of a place's history over the capricious forces of the present.

During their two visits to the Linden Hotel in June 1999 and October 2000, the SEMGHS became well acquainted with the ghosts of Linden's past. One of the most dramatic images that the SEMGHS has ever captured on camera was taken by Brenda Mikulka in the hotel. "The picture is of a girl's ghost," Brad says, "she has blonde hair and is dressed in a white nightgown and is standing on her tiptoes; it's pretty amazing, one of the local papers in Linden printed it." The photograph is also posted on the SEMGHS website, where the figure and face of a girl is visible in an ectoplasmic mist.

That wasn't all. "There's this room off the bar area where the DJ has all his sound equipment," Brad explains. "Brenda went into the DJ booth when we were upstairs and was suddenly stricken ill."

The Linden Hotel, built in the 19th century, is home to the ghostly Chuck and an unidentified female spirit.

She would later tell Brad that she felt like some large, invisible presence was flying around her, doing circles through the air at a high speed—she could practically feel the breeze as it brushed by her. Hit with intense vertigo, Brenda was unable to stomach the extreme sense of motion and quickly left the room. Jack, the owner of the sports bar, was not surprised when Brenda came stumbling out of the booth, shocked and dazed. "Yup," the proprietor said to the SEMGHS team crowded around Brenda, "I know who's in that room—he's been around for a while."

Jack smiled as he asked the assembled team, "Why don't you go in there and tell me who it is?" One of the SEMGHS psychics walked into the room without hesitation; she was back out a few minutes later. "His name is Charles," she announced, "but his friends call him Chuck."

It turned out that Chuck was a regular at the Linden Hotel during its heyday, spending most of his nights carousing in the place. The haunted DJ booth used to be his bedroom when the second floor was still used for guests. Chuck's spirit is numbered among that less-common breed of ghost that is happy to haunt its chosen ground. Chuck is Linden's resident friendly ghost, remaining behind in the old hotel because he loved the place that much when he was living. The SEMGHS psychic who walked into the room received a straightforward response when she asked Chuck why he wouldn't cross over. "It's simple," she told Brad after communicating with the spirit, "he enjoys it here."

As for the girl in white whom Brenda captured on camera, Brad's psychics informed him that sometime in the 1800s, she was involved in a romantic affair with one of the hotel's regular patrons (not Chuck). Whatever dreams of the future she and her paramour entertained were smothered one night when a fire erupted from the small wood-burning stove in her room and she died in her sleep of smoke inhalation. The SEMGHS has been able to detect and identify the spirit of this young woman, but why she continues to drift through the building's halls long after both she and her lover have died is anybody's guess.

Chuck and this young woman seem to be the most prominent spirits in the Linden Hotel, but there is evidence of others. During the October investigation, Brenda had spotted shadows moving under the door of the men's restroom. Knowing that there was no one in there, she swung open the door and took a picture of the empty bathroom. A few seconds later, a single orb was shining from the digital screen on her camera.

While the spirits have rarely interfered with day-to-day business in the Linden Hotel, there has been the occasional incident. Brad witnessed a glass shatter in the bartender's hand for no reason. EMF readings were taken seconds later, and the numbers that came back were much higher than normal. It is odd that the spirits in the building possess this kind of force yet restrain themselves from visiting too much terror on the people who frequent the hotel. Could the spirits have some sort of respect for a place they had so many good times in when they were living? Or are they merely indifferent to the ephemeral interactions of the mortals who cohabit the hotel with them?

Haunted House in Troy

Most of the SEMGHS's investigations are conducted in houses, not cemeteries, and while Brad Mikulka is often obliged to keep the findings of these forays secret, investigations that take place in the confines of people's homes almost always offer more intimate contact with spirits than do studies of the wide-open spaces in cemeteries. Perhaps hauntings in houses are usually the result of some tragic mortal circumstances specific to people who lived in the homes, whereas the largely nameless energies haunting cemeteries are there only because that is the resting place of their material remains. However, every generalization has its exceptions. Many gravesite ghosts do have well-documented histories, and a few such stories are recounted here. But for the most part, the ghosts that haunt houses are those paranormal entities that are most closely linked with their human pasts—those that have identifiable histories, purposes or possessions that keep them here in some form even after they have passed on.

Such was the case for a house in Troy that an SEMGHS team investigated a few days after Brad returned from the Mason cemetery. An SEMGHS member named Nick Sikes called Brad about strange things that were happening in the place he was renting.

After catching fleeting movements out of the corner of his eyes several times, Nick decided to start carrying a camera around with him at home. These glimpses usually happened when he was lying on the couch, just as his mind was wobbling over that line that separates sleep from consciousness. Moments before his head dropped,

Nick would catch dark shadows moving quickly across the hall—causing him to bolt to his feet, suddenly awake.

The breaking point came one night when he was awakened by a strong, almost suffocating scent. Roses. It was as if a mountain of the flowers loomed just beyond his sight in the darkness of his room. That, or somebody had sprayed a dozen cans of rose-scented air freshener into the room and closed the door. Jumping out of bed and yelling into the confines of his room, Nick ordered whatever was there to get out while simultaneously snapping a shot in the darkness. Later, when he got a chance to look at the picture he had taken, there were two orbs hovering in the blackness of the photograph.

Brad organized an investigation of Nick's house as soon as he laid eyes on the two celluloid orbs Nick sent to him in the mail. Mikulka visited late in August 2001, accompanied by five other SEMGHS members: Brad's wife, Brenda, two psychics and two supernatural mediums. Brad has stated that he doesn't have a heightened sense with the supernatural, but he usually has at least two members who are more psychically gifted present during SEMGHS investigations. According to Mikulka's definitions, psychics are able to see spiritual entities more readily than most of us, while mediums are gifted in their ability to actually communicate with these ghostly beings. The entire team witnessed amazing supernatural activity on this investigation.

Not only did Brad and Brenda capture some impressive photographs at Nick's house, but the psychics and mediums were kept busy as well. For reasons that were about to be partially explained, at least two ghosts were dwelling in the

Troy household. Things got weird when the Mikulkas' digital photos, taken in complete darkness, were registering bright white areas. These photographs weren't the typical orbs; Brad wasn't sure what they were dealing with. "We had no idea how those white blurs got there; it was like somebody was standing too close to the camera when the flash went off."

In one room where the psychics were sensing a lot of activity, Brenda took a picture of the darkness, and the faint image of a human neck, shoulder and arm appeared on her digital camera. But it was not until the team wandered outside the house that the investigation took a sharp turn in the direction of the bizarre.

"Our psychics sensed a lot of activity just behind the house, where one of our mediums picked up a name: Conan. Apparently, he was a farmer from the early 1900s, and the land we were standing on used to be his farm plot." No sooner had the paranormal team gleaned this information than one of the psychics suddenly felt a sharp pain move up her left arm and into her chest. A series of images flooded through the woman's mind and she was suddenly aware of that farmer's last moments of life: the last thing the farmer felt before he died was that same sharp pain in his arm and chest. He was resting against a tree that still stood in the backyard when a number of snakes leapt up at him and bit his arm. Severely startled by the striking serpents, Conan suffered a lethal heart attack, and he died right there under the tree.

Brenda took a picture of the tree in the yard, and sure enough, there in the digital display of her camera was the partial apparition of a man, just like the shot of the neck, arm and shoulder taken inside the house. It became clear that Conan, who was still sitting by the tree, was a soul completely lost. The SEMGHS was determined to help.

One of the mediums in the yard asked Conan, "Do you see a light? There are people who you know and love that will come and get you and take you into the light." The farmer responded that yes, there were actually eight "lights" hovering near him. At that moment, Brenda Mikulka took a picture of the tree; there in the photograph were eight orbs of light floating next to a white mist. The medium then helped Conan to pass over to the other side. "Go with them into the light, you'll be at peace," she said. Brad snapped about five pictures a few moments later and there was nothing there but the old tree in the night; it seems that Conan's soul finally did cross over.

Another spirit that resided with Nick in the Troy house didn't seem to be in such a rush to get to the afterlife. In fact, Nick could only stare in shock when one of the mediums called out his grandfather's name while communicating with one of the house's ghosts. It seems that his grandfather's spirit, still protective over his grandson, was keeping close watch over him. This explained Nick's recurring feelings that he was not alone, even when there was nobody else in the room, and made sense of the light blurs and discolorations that hovered over his shoulder in numerous photographs through much of his life. While Conan could only find peace when he joined the spirits of the dead, Nick's grandfather did not want to leave the land of the living. Thus the SEMGHS investigation in Troy was concluded…guiding one lost soul into the light and reuniting another man with the spirit of his grandfather.

Chapter 2

Mysterious Michigan
Legends

★ ★ ★

Though the past is always receding in time, it never really goes away. Just as we, as individuals, are shaped largely by our past experiences, so too does our society exist as an evolution of ideas and action over time. What is our culture but an accumulation of the general beliefs, assumptions and popular expressions that have developed over the course of our history?

The idea that "past is present," however, takes on a completely different meaning where Michigan's supernatural legends are concerned. For woven into the tumultuous history of the Great Lakes State are a number of ghostly tales that have survived over time. What sets the stories in the following chapter apart from the rest of the book is their historical backdrop. They are set in times and places central to what Michigan was and is. Not only are these ghostly beings rooted in significant events of the state's history, sightings of them continue to be reported to this very day, a solid …if unsettling… demonstration of how the past repeatedly comes back to haunt us.

Oath of the Hundred Heads

Late in the 1700s, a solitary log cabin stood deep within a thick forest of elm, ash and cottonwood trees just west of Lake Erie in what is now Monroe County. A hunter named Bill Quick lived in this cabin with his father, eking out an austere existence in the feral woodland. There was a rough settlement nearby, but both of the Quick men were known to shun the crude society of the frontier and rarely fraternized with others who inhabited the area. Indeed, besides the local Indians—whom the white men in the region tended to steer clear of—the company that father and son provided each other was the pair's only anchor to humanity amid the boundless wilderness of the Michigan forests.

So the murder of the elder Quick had a devastating impact on his son.

It happened one day while Bill was out hunting. A band of Indians raided his cabin and tomahawked his father, leaving the old man to die on the roughhewn floor, a large chunk of his scalp cruelly stripped from his head. The gruesome sight greeted Bill when he returned home and was burned into his mind forever. What little tenderness in the man's heart had survived the frontier was quashed in that instant. His eyes lit with homicidal fury, and he made a vow that day that would strip his soul of grace and send him down the agonizing road to madness.

Crumpling next to his father's bleeding corpse, Bill vowed vengeance. Through tears of rage he swore to take 100 Indian lives before he died, and the hunter dedicated the rest of his life to this macabre pursuit. He went about the business carefully, with the composed deliberation of an expert huntsman. Stalking Indians through the dense wood, he would strike only unaccompanied prey, inching towards his ultimate goal one man at a time. After he killed his quarry with a single bullet through the heart, the hunter would remove the head from his victim, put the gruesome memento in his satchel and take it home, where he placed it on one of the shelves that lined his walls.

The Potawatomi and Wyandot in the region were at a loss. They could not effectively retaliate because they did not know who was littering the forest with the headless bodies of their tribesmen. Noting that lone men were the only ones being killed, the Indians in the area began taking precautions, and as the years went by fewer and fewer of their number dared walk the woods alone.

The killing became more difficult as the Indians became more cautious, but Bill became only more vigilant, and as the years passed, he lost himself entirely in the hunt. Not one to socialize much in the first place, Bill became ever-more reclusive as the collection of heads in his cabin grew. The townsfolk whispered about the madness in his eyes, about the ceaseless, senseless muttering, and everyone gave him wide berth whenever he came into town for ammunition and gunpowder. Even his son, Tom.

Tom Quick never did get along with his father. His mother had passed away during his birth, and his maternal grandmother raised him. Not at all suited to the severe lifestyle of his dad, Tom was a relaxed young man with an easy disposition who lived for creature comforts. And while the tiny frontier settlement he called home was hardly the lap of luxury, the conditions were pure extravagance compared to his father's one-room cabin out in the woods.

Convinced that Tom was an indolent weakling with no interest in hunting, Bill scarcely gave him any thought through most of his life. Little did he know that the fulfillment of his life's work would one day rest on Tom's frail shoulders.

Tom was surprised, to say the least, when he got word that his father wished to see him. Supposedly, the old man had been stricken ill, and some trappers passing by his cabin had heard him wailing his son's name. While the youngest Quick had nothing in common with Bill, he did respect his father's strength and had always been eager for approval that never came. He hoped that he might be able to please his father or at the very least make amends with the old man while he was on his deathbed. Thus Tom ventured deep into the woods, growing evermore uneasy at the ugly funk of death that hung in the air as he got closer to his father's cabin. By the time he was at the door of the innocent-looking log house, the stench of rot was so thick he could barely breathe.

He opened the door—and the sight inside made him swoon with horror. All four walls were lined with shelves loaded with human heads in varying states of decomposition. While some were grinning skulls, long since stripped of any distinguishing tissue, other heads still gaped in deathly repose, their mortal features made hideous by a combination of burrowing maggots and the chemistry of putrefaction. Bill Quick lay in a bed in the middle of the room, wheezing painfully and staring at his son with feverish eyes.

The old man called him over, and Tom slowly walked towards his father on trembling legs. He barely managed to find his tongue. "Y-y-yes, Father?" the young man croaked.

Bill told his hideous life's story to his son—of his father's murder, of his vow of vengeance, of his lifelong obsession to collect 100 Indian heads.

Tom looked on in disbelief, his gaze shifting from where his father lay to the shelves with their diligently arranged rows of heads. He was not able to grasp why his father chose him, after all these years of silence, to unburden upon. "Would you like to me to bring a priest, Father?" he quivered.

"I'm not confessing, you idiot," Bill snapped at his son in irritation. "You're here because sickness has claimed me before I was able to finish. There are only 99 heads—I'm one man short of 100."

Tom stared in incomprehension.

"The duty falls on you," Bill continued, "to fulfill my oath and kill the last Indian. Only then will I be at peace."

Almost instinctively, Tom began moving back on his heels, shaking his head in terrified awe. "I'm not a killer, Father," he stammered, "I'm sorry, but I can't do this for you."

"Can't?" the old man roared from his bed, "You will, or I swear on all that is unholy that you will live to regret it."

By now, Tom was making a headlong dash for the door while his livid father started foaming in rage. Bill's parting words rang in Tom's head as the young man slammed the door shut and ran through the woods. "If you do not do as I ask, I will return from the grave to seek you out." The dying man's bloodcurdling shrieks echoed over the trees as he thundered his son's name, and Tom broke into a manic sprint, screaming at the top of his lungs in a vain attempt to drown out his father's voice. Bill Quick died later that day.

Tom's life went bad after the meeting. He tried forgetting the exchange at the cabin by losing himself in drink, but he was no longer a jolly drunk. He saw his father around every corner, in every shadow, glaring at him with terrifying malevolence, reminding him of his neglected duty.

It was not long before young Quick crumpled under the weight of his father's hateful specter. During fits of petrified inebriation, he would babble about the meeting in the cabin and the gruesome debt he owed Bill's ghost. Word got out that harmless Tom Quick was under a supernatural oath to kill an Indian, and the local settlers soon added the label of village idiot to his already distinguished title of town drunk. He quickly became the laughing stock of the community—consistently ridiculed, especially when an Indian came into town. "Here's your chance, Tom!" someone would shout. "Get to work, Quick! Your dad's coming!"

Tom had endured two years of this nightmarish torment before a late-night visit in autumn wiped out what little was left of his sanity. He was trying to get to sleep one cold, clear October night when the door to his cabin was violently flung open. In the stream of moonlight that flooded into Tom's one-room cabin stood the rotting corpse of Bill Quick, his hunting rifle in hand. Tom stared in speechless horror as the undead ghoul brandished his rifle and shrieked savagely. An inhuman voice emerged from the tortured corpse's decayed lips, ordering his detested son to kill the 100th Indian so that he and his own father could finally rest. If he did not do so by the following midnight, Bill threatened that he would come back with Tom's murdered grandfather.

That night, Tom was seen running through the streets of town, knocking on every door he passed, begging hysterically for refuge. Garbling unintelligibly through frenzied tears about his father's corpse, the unfulfilled oath and his impending doom, it was obvious to everyone he encountered that he had gone completely mad.

His frantic search for help continued on through the next day, but everyone steered clear of him, wishing to have nothing to do with the ranting lunatic. The last time anyone would see Tom alive, he was plunging into the woods just as dusk was falling, tearing down the road that led to his father's cabin.

It was afternoon the next day when some of the men in town decided to go looking for him, fully expecting to find Tom dead somewhere in the forest. Tom's trail led the search party to the door of Bill Quick's cabin. Ever since the hunter had died, people tended to stay away from the solitary lodging, sensing something foreboding about the place.

On this day, the men who went after Tom would discover why. Pushing open the door into the log hut, the men gazed in mute terror at the skulls still displayed in perfect rows along the walls of the room. And on the space reserved for the last skull was Tom Quick's freshly decapitated head, staring at the horror-struck party with a look of incomprehensible agony. His body was nowhere to be found.

Candlelight on 24th Street

It was in 1760 in the midst of all the bloodshed during the French and Indian War that a single man performed a small act of compassion that flew in the face of the brutal visage of armed conflict. Where French, Indian and English visited merciless death on each other in the cities, farms and woods of colonial America, an Englishman near Fort Detroit adopted an orphaned Indian girl as his own. It happened not long after the English captured Detroit in 1760; a mill keeper in the settlement surrounding the fort defied the popular British attitudes towards the Indians of the area and took in a young Indian girl whose family had fallen victim to the misfortunes of war. The girl's foster-father raised her as if she were his own child, bringing her up with European customs and values. But she would not be able to leave her past behind completely.

A young Ottawa brave named Wasson did not think much of the English occupants in Detroit and took it on himself to watch over the girl from a distance. Wasson's protective feelings for her turned to love as the Indian girl grew to adulthood. Despite the warnings from other braves in his tribe to leave the young woman alone, that her upbringing among the whites in Detroit had smothered her Indian roots, Wasson could not deny his passion. And though he never did approach her, he watched over her from afar with a covetous eye, tormented by the demons of an unattainable love.

The watchful days of his vigil turned to manic stalking at night when Wasson learned that the girl had fallen in love. Whenever the mill owner was away, the girl would stand before her window with a lit candle, signaling to her lover who was waiting in the surrounding trees. In another moment, a dark figure wrapped in a military coat would emerge from the bush and make his way into the mill. A hot wave of jealous rage washed over Wasson when he discovered that the man was none other than Colonel Campbell, one of the leading English military men at Fort Detroit.

While the 1763 Treaty of Paris officially ended the French and Indian War, a document signed by statesmen on another continent meant little to the Indians in the Great Lakes region. The major difference for the Ottawas, Wyandots, Potawatomis and Ojibwas in the area was that the French trading posts in the area were now occupied by English; it was a change that they were not at all happy with. Over the decades, French traders had developed close relationships with Indians through fur traders and missionaries, whereas the Anglophones who now occupied the string of forts from Michilimackinac to Detroit to Vincennes were almost intolerably arrogant.

Just as the peace was being drafted between the English and French in Paris, many of the Great Lakes Indians became convinced that they could no longer suffer the English expansion into their territory. The great Ottawa war chief, Pontiac, was marshalling braves from the surrounding tribes and was about to go on the warpath against the hated English.

Wasson could not fathom how this girl, a woman of his people, could be consorting with the Ottawas' sworn enemy, and the brave's blind desire for this same girl turned his anger into a murderous fury. Just as Pontiac was planning his attack on Fort Detroit, the lovesick Wasson schemed up a sortie of his own, and on a dark, moonless night, he crept into the young woman's room and murdered her.

Pontiac's allies managed to take the British outposts at Michilimackinac, Sandusky and Presque Isle. Terror erupted along the western borders of Virginia, Maryland and Pennsylvania as countless settlements were attacked along the frontier. But Pontiac's own surprise attack on Detroit was foiled, and he never was able to take the fort in the bloody fighting over the next several months.

Wasson's fate during the Indian uprising is unknown, yet the young woman he killed left an indelible mark on Detroit's history. Shortly after the murder, settlers passing by the mill at night could see the image of the slain Indian maiden standing in front of the window with a lit candle, blankly staring at them as they walked by. People shunned the building as word of the haunting spread, and in an attempt to rid the town of her ghost, the old mill, dilapidated and abandoned, was torn down in 1795.

Yet sightings of the solitary woman with the candle persisted. Even today, some say they have seen a beautiful young woman walking along Detroit's waterfront on 24th Street—vainly looking for her long-dead colonel.

The First Ghost Ship on the Great Lakes

If he ever stopped to think about it, René-Robert Cavelier, Sieur de La Salle, would have been quite certain that he was making history. An empire builder and fortune hunter, La Salle was among the first of the Europeans to venture into America's interior, claiming as the property of King Louis of France every territory, waterway and beast that he saw. He made his way into America by way of the Great Lakes, the Mississippi, the Illinois and the Ohio rivers, engineering a considerable French presence in forts along the Mississippi's tributaries and the basin of the great river itself and christening the humid, arable region "Louisiana."

Though La Salle did have the French king's official sanction in his explorations, he did not have the crown's financial support, and accumulated debts soon threatened the young adventurer's ambitions. During a stint of monetary desperation, hoping to finance his exploration down the Mississippi with revenue generated by fur-trading excursions, La Salle oversaw the construction of a trading ship on Lake Erie. Completed in 1679, the single sail 45-ton *Griffon* would be the first commercial ship to be launched on that lake. But the ship would not complete a single journey on the rough waters of the Great Lakes.

On August 7, 1679, La Salle took the *Griffon* on its maiden voyage up the Detroit River, through Lake St. Clair, right over Lake Huron and into Lake Michigan. The French explorer docked in Green Bay, loaded his ship with furs and ordered "Luke the Dane," the hulking ship captain, to deliver the cargo to Niagara before the end of the year. But the first European commercial ship built on the Great Lakes was also destined to become the first of many commercial ships that would founder in those waters. The ship and all its precious cargo would never reach Niagara. It would never, in fact, be seen again, at least not in corporeal form…

There are numerous tales about what may have happened to the ship during its ill-fated journey to Niagara that fall. One story is that a group of Indians warned the ship's crew to wait out a coming storm while anchored in northern Lake Michigan. Unimpressed by the warnings, Luke reportedly responded with a careless snort. He gave the order to tack against the wind, and the *Griffon* pushed past the Straits of Mackinac, forever to be lost somewhere in Huron's tempestuous waters.

Another story tells the tale of the men revolting against their captain—with a mutinying crew pitching the Dane overboard and making for a faraway port with La Salle's beaver pelts. Or were they boarded by a group of hostile Indians? This version of the *Griffon*'s fate has the entire ship's crew massacred and the vessel stripped of its cargo, set loose to drift to its doom somewhere on Lake Huron.

Whatever happened to the *Griffon*, experts in the region's folklore all agree that it is the oldest ghost ship on the Great Lakes. Over the years, there have been numerous sightings of a pale ship during especially violent storms on Lake Michigan's northern waters. It is a bone white, slightly transparent ship—impossibly antiquated—with a tattered single sail set full and the words *Le Griffon* etched across the fore of the hull. Whenever concerned ship captains have attempted to approach the old vessel to offer succor from the storm, it has vanished into thin air, the rolling waters and howling winds of unforgiving Michigan betraying no sign that it was ever there at all.

The Red Dwarf

The first people to settle Detroit called him "Le Nain Rouge," a grotesque little hobgoblin standing no more than 2 feet tall with glaring red eyes and warty crimson skin burning under a coarse blanket of thick black hair. If observers were not sure whether to be afraid or amused by the shambling little horror, they soon learned that the Red Dwarf was a faithful predecessor of calamity. Without fail, disaster followed close behind any appearance of the hideous gnome. Almost every notable misfortune in Detroit—from the ruin of Antoine de la Mothe Cadillac in the 18th century to the devastating ice storm of 1976—fell soon after a sighting of this stumpy monstrosity.

According to legend, the first European to encounter the Red Dwarf was Cadillac, the founder of Detroit City. The famous French explorer was sitting on the bank of the Detroit River some time in the early 1700s, blithely watching the water flow by, when the Red Dwarf jumped down from one of the surrounding trees and landed right in front of the startled Frenchman. The Dwarf was giggling uncontrollably as bubbling tendrils of drool dripped from the rancid leer on its face. Leaping from one foot to the next in a demented dance, it wielded a tree branch like a sword, coming at Cadillac with exaggerated lunges and ridiculous

The Red Dwarf

parries. Cadillac would have surely laughed at this clownish display of swordsmanship if the little creature were not so alarmingly repugnant. Drawing his sword and beating the brownie back with the flat of his blade, Cadillac stared in wonder as the Red Dwarf turned and ran, its mad cackle trailing off as it disappeared into the woods.

Soon after his encounter with the Red Dwarf, Cadillac's fortunes plummeted, and his schemes to make Detroit the "Paris of New France" failed. Arrogant and overly ambitious, he upset the interests of established traders in Montreal, angered the Governor of New France and made enemies of the Jesuits. Cadillac was recalled to France in 1710, losing his trade monopoly out of Detroit and all the privileges that went with it.

The next time a sighting of the Red Dwarf was recorded, it was 1763, and the American colonies were in the throes of open warfare as the English, French and their respective Indian allies fought for dominance of the continent. On July 30 of that year, the settlers spotted the Red Dwarf near the Detroit River, giggling to itself while doing cartwheels along the river's banks. About 24 hours later, one of Pontiac's war parties decimated a force at Parent's Creek, killing 60 men and their commanding officer at the Battle of Bloody Run.

It was about 40 years later, late in the spring of 1805, when the Red Dwarf was seen again. Several people spotted the stunted fiend hobbling through Detroit's back streets, cackling in deranged glee. All who saw the dwarf that day did their best to get as far away from the monster as they could, but just as before, disaster followed in the Red Dwarf's footsteps. On June 11 of that year, a fire started in the local baker's stable. Spreading to the surrounding buildings, the blaze was soon raging out of control; it ravaged the entire town before it ran its course, burning practically everything to the ground.

Old General William Hull, the only officer in American history to be sentenced to death for military incompetence, claimed that he saw the Red Dwarf grinning at him from the fog on the fateful day in 1813 that he surrendered Detroit to the invading British army. His fellow officers and the public at large were outraged by his cowardly capitulation, given that the garrison in Detroit outnumbered the British force. He was court-martialed under charges of cowardice and neglect of duty and condemned to death. Though he eventually received a presidential pardon from James Madison, he never outlived the humiliation of his court-martial. To the end of his days, poor Will Hull was haunted by the Red Dwarf's burning red eyes piercing through the thick fog drifting off Lake St. Clair.

And there is reason to believe that the Red Dwarf yet lives. Just before Detroit police raided the United Community and Civic League—an illegal after-hours bar—late in July 1967, the Red Dwarf was said to have been dashing down 12th Street, doing back flips and cartwheels as he ran. In a matter of hours, 12th Street would become the terrible epicenter of the week-long racial riots that erupted after the police raid. When the smoke cleared on July 30, 43 people had been killed, 7000 arrested, and property damage was estimated at about $22 million. The Detroit riots were the worst bout of urban violence that the United States experienced during the tumultuous 1960s.

Two linemen were on their lunch break on March 1, 1976, when they saw what they thought was a child shimmying up a utility pole. Yelling at the mischievous creature to get down from its perch, they were horrified at the sight that greeted them when the little offender slid down. It wasn't a child; it wasn't even human. The Red Dwarf leered at the two city workers before dashing off, making remarkable time with its absurdly lopsided gait. Not a day later, Detroit was hit by the worst ice storm in its history, destroying power lines and leaving nearly 400,000 Detroit residents without electricity.

Since that time, Detroit's inverted version of the Irish leprechaun has been reclusive. Though it has been claimed that people have spotted the truncated harbinger of doom before falling to personal tragedies, there have been no accounts since 1976 of the Red Dwarf preceding public disasters. For instance, there were no Red Dwarf sightings before the ice storm in 1997, which did more damage than the storm in 1976.

Has the ancient imp finally succumbed to age? Has somebody seized the agile dwarf and broken the adage that discourages one from shooting the messenger? Has Le Nain Rouge just up and left, deciding that Detroit has gotten too crowded for its liking? Or even yet, is it simply waiting for disaster of a scope deserving of its presence? Surely then, going by historical precedent, if the 2-foot demon is still kicking around…it is best that no one is able to confirm it.

The Crouch Murders

Every year, some time between dusk on November 21 and dawn on November 22, the ghost of the long-departed Eunice White makes her way through the streets of Jackson, Michigan, moving down Reynolds Road until it intersects with Horton past the southwest limits of the city. There she turns into the abandoned Reynolds cemetery, where long-crumbling headstones fight a losing battle against encroaching roots and overgrown weeds. The apparition of Eunice White, a vague human shape surrounded by a dense spot of fog, hesitates for a moment at the cemetery gates before entering. She always takes the same path, deliberately drifting through the rows of unkempt tombstones to stop in front of the one she is looking for. The ghost hovers there for a few moments until a single breeze gently drifts through her and she dissipates into the wind, leaving no trace that she was ever there. As always, the granite tombstone that is the focus of her attention is that of Jacob Crouch, 1809–83.

Eunice White and Jacob Crouch were two casualties in one of the ugliest tragedies in Jackson's past. It happened in 1883 when the city of Jackson was still a small agricultural and mining community—not yet 50 years old. The town was rocked by a string of hideous murders that would scar it forever.

It all started on the evening of November 21, when a violent storm was passing over Jackson County. Torrential rain thundered down on residents' roofs while a number of lightning strikes incinerated trees and destroyed a few farm buildings. Whatever anxieties Jackson's citizens felt as they huddled in their homes under the roaring chaos of the storm above was nothing compared to what was happening over at Jacob Crouch's place.

Everybody staying at the Crouch farm was murdered that night, including 74-year-old Jacob Crouch, his daughter Eunice White, who was nine months pregnant, her husband Henry White and Moses Polley, a 24-year-old man visiting from out of town. All were found lying in their blood-soaked sheets, apparently shot to death while they slept. There was no trace of the killer, or killers, responsible for the massacre.

But whoever had turned the house into a deathtrap was not finished with the Crouch family just yet. Not two months later, on January 2, 1884, Jacob Crouch's one surviving daughter, Susan Halcomb, was found dead on the floor of her bedroom. Someone had apparently force-fed her a lethal dose of poison. The bizarre killing spree continued when James Fay, a former farmhand for Jacob Crouch, was murdered shortly after Susan. The last man to fall was Susan's husband. It was not certain whether he had committed suicide or was murdered as well, but his demise did mark the last of the deaths that had afflicted the community of Jackson.

Several men were brought to trial for the six murders but no one was convicted, and the Crouch killings would go unpunished, leaving a serial killer—or perhaps a number of killers—to grow old peacefully somewhere in the United States, maybe right in Jackson. Yet the incident would not fade quietly into Jackson's past.

Eunice White was buried in St. John's Cemetery in Jackson, and Jacob Crouch was buried in Reynolds Cemetery, a tiny graveyard about 5 miles away from St. John's. While the people of Jackson noticed the patch of cloud that drifted

The ghost of Eunice White continues to visit her father's tombstone.

down Reynolds Road on November 1884, the phenomenon fell into that category of inexplicable occurrences that people feel are best forgotten. But as the years went by, it became obvious that this apparition would always be seen on the same road and on the same night, November 21, every year.

Of course the Crouch murders still loomed large in citizens' minds, and it was not long before the ghost was linked to the killings. A few years later when several witnesses saw the cloud materialize over Eunice White's grave and make its way to Jacob Crouch's burial site in Reynolds Cemetery, the mystery of the apparition's identity was considered solved—or solved to a certain extent anyway.

The popular assumption is that Eunice's ghost makes her way to her father's tombstone on the anniversary of their murder out of some kind of filial affection. Maybe the fact that her father is buried in another cemetery makes her unable to see him in the afterlife, and she makes her way to Reynolds every year because she misses him. Or perhaps she witnessed her father's suffering in the last moments of his life, and the experience left such an impression on her soul that part of her will always be bound to his material remains.

But what if Eunice is trying to say something with her annual pilgrimage to her father's grave? It is true that her killer (or killers) were never brought to justice. Perhaps her soul will never be able to rest until the case has been solved, and her yearly trip to Reynolds Cemetery is some kind of clue to a murder case that has long since been relegated to history. Like everything else about the Crouch murders, Eunice's purpose may forever remain a mystery. And we can only hope that one day Eunice's soul finds peace.

Zoe and Sebastian

Lost love and undying loyalty. One of Detroit's most persisting ghost stories is a tale of uncompromising fidelity, of a passionate devotion so extraordinary that it defied the monolithic wall of mortality over 100 years ago and reportedly still endures today—coming to life with every spring thaw of the Detroit River.

It was back when Michigan was an immense stretch of woodland, populated mostly by Chippewas, Ottawas and Potawatomi. Detroit was only a military fort, surrounded by a cluster of Indian settlements, and most of the men in the region made their living trapping a seemingly limitless supply of beaver from the vast hinterland. It was in this hard world that a fur trapper named Sebastian met and courted a beautiful young woman named Zoe, and the two made a passionate vow to marry in the coming spring.

But the long winter season still stood between them as Sebastian readied himself for his journey to the far-off northern country to man his traplines. Fur trapping was difficult, dangerous work and Sebastian eased Zoe's troubled mind with a fervent promise: "Dead or alive, hell or high water, I'll be back down the Detroit as soon as the ice leaves the lakes."

For Zoe, the long winter was almost unendurable. As early as January, she began going down to the banks of the Detroit River every day, anxiously looking for signs of the spring thaw. Staring out on the frozen body of water, her mind wandered over the icy layers of the Great Lakes and into the snow-covered forests of Michigan, to where her lover was as he went about the grueling work along his

*Sebastian paddled into destiny, never to return
to Zoe except in spirit form once a year every year.*

traplines. Days turned to weeks, which turned to months, and finally, on one misty April morning, her impatient eyes looked upon the large blocks of ice break up drifting down from Lake St. Clair and Lake Huron. Spring had arrived.

And on that same morning, she looked out on the river with almost delirious happiness as the figure of Sebastian came out of the fog, steering his fur-laden canoe to where she stood. Yet as he drew closer, his image began to fade in front of her very eyes…the canoe and its bountiful cargo started evaporating into mist, and Sebastian himself was becoming more and more transparent. Just before he disappeared completely, Zoe heard his last promise echo in the crisp morning air: "Dead or alive, hell or high water, I'll be back down the Detroit as soon as the ice leaves the lakes."

Zoe would return to the river's bank on that day every April for the rest of her life. And on that day, the ghostly form of Sebastian would reappear, rowing down the Detroit in his loaded canoe before fading again into the mist of the early morning…that same vow drifting faintly to the river's edge. It is said that to this very day, if you are standing at the right place at the right time, you can still see Sebastian rowing through the floating blocks of ice, fulfilling his last earthly promise to Zoe.

Chapter 3

Phantoms in Public

★ ★ ★

*For the most part, ghosts haunt private places. The extreme circum-
stances that are usually attached to lingering spirits appear to be akin
to the idiosyncrasies of individuals: haunts, like people, appear to
be more comfortable finding expression behind closed doors,
in the safety of their homes. But not always.*

*There are those ghosts that have no qualms sharing their
supernatural foibles with the general population. Unlike
haunted houses, which affect a smaller number of people,
these public hauntings are usually widely reported within the
county they occur. Whether proprietors like it or not, their businesses
often become associated with the ghosts that haunt them,
and it is these buildings which most readily become paranormal
landmarks among enthusiasts. If the reader were to inquire about
ghosts with a town local, these are the stories that would most
probably emerge. It is these tales that are woven
into the fabric of Michigan.*

The Paulding Light

The Robbins Lake Road winds through the woods of the Upper Peninsula between two quiet northern towns, Paulding and Watersmeet. Follow the road to the top of a hill about a half-mile west of US 45. From this vantage point, you will find a barricade blocking the inconspicuous back road, a sign put up by the Forest Service and, on any summer evening, a crowd of observers standing around their cars, eagerly scanning the sky for the famous Paulding Light.

The Light has been documented by scientists and paranormal experts alike. It elicits all sorts of reactions, from rational theories regarding swamp gas, mineral deposits, reflecting light and electromagnetic energy to supernatural explanations that involve the lingering spirit of a murdered postal worker, a dead railroad brakeman, a broken-hearted engineer or doughy old Pancake Joe.

Most observers lean towards the supernatural explanations. The Forest Service itself endorses the most unscientific of answers with the placard it erected at the site (see p. 107).

Yet the ghost of the dead brakeman is only one legend among many. Other storytellers assert that the multi-colored glow that dances after dusk is indeed a lantern, but it belongs to a railroad engineer, not a brakeman. This version contends that an engineer in Ontonagon County confronted a lewd lumberjack in a local pub over rumors the logger was spreading about his one-and-only. The engineer was stabbed in the ensuing fight and died later that night. After he was buried, it become known that the stories the lumberjack was telling were actually true, that the late engineer's sweetheart was in

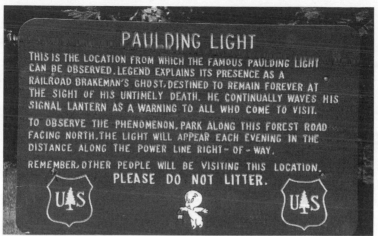

The Paulding Light sign

fact unfaithful. So it is said that the ghost of the engineer still wanders the woods around Paulding, looking for his own soul, lost by the treachery of his one true love. And the Paulding Light is the lantern he carries when he goes on his nightly searches.

Another folktale involves one of the state's earliest postal workers, who traded in his horse for a dogsled when working his route during Michigan's snowbound winter months. On a cold January morning, a local hunter's grisly discovery explained why the people in the region had not been getting any letters lately. There, amid the wreck of a dogsled and scattered mail that had yet to be delivered, lay the corpse of the postman and what was left of his sled team. The bodies of master and dogs alike were frozen stiff in gruesome poses of untimely death, strewn across a stretch of blood red snow, their throats slit open from ear to ear. The region has been called Dog Meadow ever since, and some people believe that the Paulding Light is the murdered mailman, coming back every night to get his team together.

There is also the story of Pancake Joe, a big man who ran a saloon in Watersmeet and ended up buying a rock farm near Paulding. If it is indeed Pancake Joe's spirit on Robbins Lake Road, it was not a traumatic death, but firmly held convictions, that caused Joe to linger on in Michigan after his death. Pancake Joe was a man who shunned civilization and fought the settlement of America's hinterlands to the very end. His temper went bad after power lines went through the area, and he died soon after. This theory has the spirit of Pancake Joe climbing the electric poles and dancing along the lines, sending sparks flying—a tireless attempt to frighten people away from the secluded land that he knew and loved.

The phenomenon of mysterious lights appearing in the night is not isolated to Paulding. Dancing flashes of red, white, yellow and green lights have been documented in other places, and observers taken to calling them "earth lights" have tried to attach rational explanations for their existence. Whatever the case, in sub-zero temperatures of the frigid Michigan winter or balmy evenings of Michigan's summer months, the Paulding Light continues to shine, attracting scientific observers, paranormal enthusiasts and undecided onlookers alike.

The Bower's Harbor Inn

While sudden death, dramatic circumstances and heartrending tragedy lie at the root of many hauntings, some spirits linger on past death because they are fervently attached to objects of the material world. A great number of haunted houses happen to be magnificent old homes—perhaps the people who built the homes so loved them that they cannot get themselves to leave, even after death intervenes.

This might very well be the case for Bower's Harbor Inn near Traverse City. The mansion was built by J.W. Stickney and his wife Genevive in the late 19th century. The Stickneys were an ambitious couple captivated by the natural beauty of Old Mission Peninsula. A scenic stretch of land that juts out into Grand Traverse Bay, the mile-and-a-half wide peninsula is adorned with sandy beaches and lush oak and pine forests. J.W. and Genevive made their home in a rudimentary farmhouse when they first settled in the area. While Mr. Stickney was busy making inroads in the lumber and steel businesses, Genevive's farm-fresh preserves, jams and brandies began to make her famous among the locals. Before long, the couple amassed an impressive fortune and built an extravagant mansion to replace their farmhouse.

The Stickneys spent the rest of their lives on the gorgeous Old Mission estate, which continues to stand long after the original owners have passed on. Though the house changed hands a number of times after the Stickneys left, no one seems to have been able to call it home since J.W. and Genevive lived there. As attractive as the house is to all who visit, there is a sense that the place has a soul of its own, a soul not so interested in accommodating new people.

The Stickney mansion was renamed the Bower's Harbor Inn when Jim and Fern Bryant bought the place in 1959 and converted it into a restaurant. They warned Toni Scharling and her two friends, Sally and Bruce Towner, that strange things were going on when the trio bought the place from them in 1964, but the new buyers were too enraptured with the scenic estate to pay the Bryants much attention. Intending to run the restaurant and make the place a home for their families, Scharling and the Towners quickly discovered that while they may have legally owned the house after they had bought it, it was actually somebody else's home.

In her book *Michigan: Haunts and Hauntings*, Marion Kuclo describes one particular mirror in Bower's Harbor Inn as being a favorite item of what is presumably the ghost of Genevive Stickney. The legend is that Genevive, who was a little bit stocky, had a gilded mirror built that would make her reflection appear thinner. She must have spent a considerable amount of time gazing into this device, because one of the most common sightings of Genevive's ghost is in this same mirror.

Soon after Toni Scharling and her friends had purchased the place, one of the patrons in the restaurant came running out of the room where Genevive's mirror was mounted. Breathless and shaking with fear, the woman practically barreled over Scharling, who was walking down the adjoining hallway at that moment.

"Good heavens!" exclaimed Toni. "Are you all right?"

The woman took a few moments to calm down before telling the proprietress what she had just seen. She had just been in the other room, enjoying the slimmed-down version of herself reflecting from the looking glass, when another woman appeared in the reflection over her shoulder. The sudden visitor definitely did not look like she subscribed to the popular fashions of the 1960s. Her hair was pulled up into a bun that was held together by an elaborate hairpin and she was dressed in a lavish evening gown. The customer turned to speak to this oddly dressed woman who had just appeared behind her, but when she spun around, there was nobody there. That was just before she had bolted out of the room and ran into Toni.

This patron would not be the last person to see a woman's apparition. Many other diners at the Bower's Harbor Inn would spot a woman standing right behind them, but when they turned around to face the woman, she had disappeared.

That was not the only ghostly activity that took place in the old mansion. The Towner and Scharling families living upstairs above the restaurant often felt like moving targets for an unseen assailant when household objects would come flying at them as if thrown by an invisible hand. There were several witnesses in the restaurant on one busy evening when a plate of food on the salad bar seemed to hurl itself off the counter and onto the floor. No one near the bar could be blamed for the mess. In the middle of the night, strange knocking sounds were heard coming from the walls, doors, or inside of closets, and doors would often fly open or slam shut when there wasn't even a trace of a breeze in the house. Family members' possessions would often go missing, eventually to be found in the oddest places days later.

Like nearly all incidents of supernatural phenomena, any attempt at explaining the causes of the event are almost purely conjecture. Perhaps traumatic events in the Stickney household left some sort of psychic imprint in parts of the house. Could it be that the spirits in the mansion are trying to say something to the living? Or maybe the Stickneys really do love their home too much to leave. Paranormal expert Marion Kuclo wrote that the house isn't even haunted by "ghosts" per se, but is afflicted by poltergeists and shades—the former a manifestation of psychic human forces, the latter a result of specific atmospheric conditions combined with historical episodes to reveal snapshots from the past. Whatever the case, the bizarre events at the Bower's Harbor Inn continued after Scharling and the Towners sold the restaurant.

Ernest Hall, manager of the restaurant in the late 70s, was not one who believed in ghosts, but he found himself relying on supernatural explanations to make sense of the happenings in the restaurant when he was running it. "During the winter months, we were only open on the weekend for the dinner hours," Mr. Hall recalls. "It was sometime past 1 AM on one of these nights and I was locking up after finishing some paperwork. I noticed that the basement lights were on just as I was leaving and went downstairs to shut them off. I was the first person back at 8 the next morning, so it took me quite by surprise to see the basement lights had been turned back on."

He went downstairs and turned the lights off before running some errands at the bank and the post office. The lights were on again when he got back. Still skeptical that anything ghostly was going on, Ernest called both the owner and the cook, the only other people who had keys to the place. They told Ernest that they had not been in since the night before. That was when he began to doubt all the little rational explanations he had invented for the strange occurrences. Perhaps the rapping on the walls wasn't mischievous guests, and what about that door to the ladies' room on the second floor that repeatedly slammed shut when there was no draft at all?

Besides the sudden national acclaim of the cuisine at Bower's Inn, not much has changed in the restaurant since Schelde Enterprises bought the place in 1974. All the incidents have been variations on the same theme: inanimate objects moving independently of any natural force. While doors throughout the house have continued to slam shut without the help of anyone or anything, the old elevator that J.W. Stickney had put in when he was too old to make it up the stairs seems to be haunted as well. Reportedly, one customer using the elevator found himself alone with an ancient J.W. when riding the lift. The elevator was eventually shut down for safety reasons, but there are a number of reports of it coming to life by itself, moving from one floor to another with no active electrical line to power its pulleys and no one on board.

The current management of the restaurant maintains that the Stickneys still reside in their old home. It seems that the stubborn spirits have even taken to a few new tricks. The building's office manager has noticed that the grandfather clock downstairs somehow moves ahead 25 minutes in the space of five minutes. The dining room candles, all left unlit at night, have been found lit first thing in the morning. Inventory clipboards set down one place have reappeared somewhere else…assuming that clipboards lack volition, it has been surmised that some mysterious trickster, of this world or another, has taken to moving them.

And so business at the Bower's Harbor Inn goes on, with the staff members doing their best to accommodate the building's original owners, who still seem set on staying put.

The Legend of Dog Lady

On a small, isolated island in east Monroe, connected to the mainland by a causeway off Dunbar Road, stands of thick vegetation cast deep shadows over the scattered detritus of human settlement. Broken lawn chairs lie next to discarded refrigerators. The innards of old, half-eaten mattresses spill onto the muddy ground as an armless doll imbedded in the dirt stares blankly at a fat wolf spider that creeps over the ground towards her. There is a loud rustling in the bush, followed by a strange, high-pitched growl; it is an eerie noise, unlike any sound made by any of God's creatures. Welcome to Dog Lady Island.

The island has been used for different purposes at different times. In the mid-19th century, Reverend Erasmus Boyd built a large two-story house there to be used as a summer retreat for students at the Monroe Young Ladies Seminary. After the minister sold the building a few years later, numerous ventures were attempted on the property—everything from a pig farm to a community for low-income earners to a sugar cane farm to a garbage dump. But ever since the Boyd house burned down in 1961, the island has become the home of one of Monroe's most lasting urban legends: the Dog Lady.

An old vagrant couple stumbled onto the tiny island not long after fire consumed Reverend Boyd's old house. Scavenging enough usable material from the old building, the two mendicants decided to settle there permanently. The area was still quite secluded, with almost no human settlement anywhere nearby, and the couple went about making a humble home away from Monroe society. Yet the husband passed away soon after he had finished building a crude house on the island, leaving the wife there to fend for herself. It was then that things went very, very wrong.

It was not that she had an unusually strong attachment to animals, but the only living things that paid the widow any mind were the stray dogs that roamed the area. Quickly growing tired of the solitude on the island, she took to feeding the beasts that came by. Most of these hounds never wandered very far after they were fed, and in a short time the woman had an entire pack of snarling, yelping mongrels for friends. Years passed, and with nothing but canine companionship, the old woman began to lose touch with her humanity. Instead of walking on two legs, she began to shuffle about on all fours. She took to barking at the animals when she wanted to communicate, growled at any dog that dared compete with her for food and howled along with the pack whenever the night was lit by a full moon.

But try as she might, she was never accepted by the other animals. She was human after all. No shaggy coat ever did grow on her back, she did not develop four paws or

The legend of the Dog Lady persists in Michigan.

grow a tail, and no sharp points grew between her incisors and her molars.

The unspeakable happened one day when the dogs were feeding on some freshly killed carcass. The old woman shambled over with her awkward four-legged gait, looking to dig her nose into some of the spoils. She angered one of the voracious animals when she came too close to its snout, and the dog lashed out at her. It was as if the hounds had been waiting for just such an attack. In a matter of seconds, the entire pack turned on her.

The dogs tore her arms and legs to ribbons, raked her face with innumerable wounds and ripped her tongue from her mouth. Though she survived the mauling, the woman was hideously mutilated by the vicious attack and from that day on kept her distance from the animals. For their part, when it became obvious that the woman could no longer supply them with food, the dogs roamed away from the island, leaving the old woman by herself once more. Yet it would not be long before her island would become the stomping grounds for packs of an entirely different sort of animal.

In the late 1960s, the drive across the causeway down Dunbar Road and into the heavily wooded island became popular among young people. Every weekend, the old woman loped away from the sounds of approaching adolescents, hiding herself in the woods and looking on as high school kids cavorted in the clearing in front of her. But she did not remain hidden from the eyes of humanity for too long. An anxious hush would fall over many of the drunken parties whenever revelers standing too close to the edge of the clearing would hear a bizarre grunt or snarl from the bush. As the parties grew more frequent, the woman grew more impatient and began creeping closer to the revelers. She would often appear in front of a lone teenager long after everyone else had fallen asleep. Hunched over on all fours, she growled menacingly through rotten teeth until the unfortunate witness would go running for the shelter of a car, wailing in fright.

She grew braver when there were fewer visitors. On nights when young couples drove out to the island for some privacy, she would interrupt their amorous exchanges by leaping up on the roof of their car, howling menacingly. As these kids peeled away from the island, they would often catch a glimpse of the woman in their headlights, shambling away wildly on feet and hands before disappearing into the woods.

So it was that this woman earned the befitting title of Dog Lady from Monroe's young inhabitants, and the place she inhabited became known as Dog Lady Island. Time passed, but the Dog Lady was ageless, and with every subsequent sighting the old woman seems to have become more and more lupine—suffering the growth of long canine teeth and dog-like ears, sprouting a long hairy snout.

Perhaps our species' grip on our humanity is not as solid as scientists may have us believe. Could it be that our behavior, thoughts and even physical appearance depend more on our immediate surroundings than some established genetic code? Maybe all it would take to turn a proud *homo sapien* into some doddering horror from H.G. Wells's imagination is prolonged exposure to another species. Witness Farley Mowat's time with wild wolves in Canada's north, and of course there are the famous stories of Tarzan and his experiences in the jungles of Africa.

Reports of the Dog Lady's physical transformation may certainly be the products of over-active imaginations, and she may be just as human today as she was in the early 1960s. Whether she has truly become half-dog, half-human, or is merely a woman who has suffered extremely bad luck, stories of the Dog Lady persist. A local bike gang called the Iron Coffins allegedly started using the island as a center of their operations during the 1970s, and kids stopped partying there. Groups of adventurous youngsters still traveled to the island, though, and it was at this time that some of them claimed they spotted a coffin tucked away in a thick copse—and that the Dog Lady herself had taken to sleeping in it. Was the coffin a gift from the bike gang? Quite likely. The Dog Lady's vicious independence may have drawn the Iron Coffins' admiration.

While there are not nearly as many parties on Dog Lady Island today as there were in the 60s, couples still park off Dunbar Road, and given the reported agility with which the Dog Lady still jumps up on the roof of these teenagers' cars, the years have taken nothing away from her. Except, possibly, more of her humanity.

A Spectral Business Partner

Mary Manning (a pseudonym) had always promised Denise Hard, her best friend and employee, that she would let Denise know what the afterlife was like when she got to the other side. Not that either of the women was obsessed with death, but those working in Mary's restaurant on 1339 Newaygo Street in the small town of Bailey often mused on the supernatural—given that Mary's deceased mother was a regular at the establishment.

There were no previous accounts of unusual activity in the old building, but when Mary opened the restaurant in 1993, a year after her mother had passed away, bizarre things began to happen. It all started about half a year after Mary had set up her new business. Denise Hard remembers the first time a kitchen appliance jumped from a shelf on its own and shattered all over the floor. After that single incident, things were never the same at the restaurant.

"As time went on more and more strange things began to happen," Denise says. Efforts to close the place up for the night, for instance, were frequently being confounded. Denise would come out of the back room after the cleaning lady had finished all her closing duties to find the place in complete disarray, with the blinds open and all the lights on.

"Or there were times," Denise recalls, "that Mary would open up in the morning when I had closed the night before so I knew how clean everything was when I left. But first thing in the morning Mary would walk in and chairs would be on their sides, salt and pepper shakers were strewn about, salt and pepper would be all over the tables, sugar packets were ripped open, and sugar was strewn all over the place."

On other occasions, it seems the ghost would try to communicate with Mary. "Some mornings she'd walk in and there was writing on the refrigerators in the back with ketchup," Denise says. The ghost did not have much to say, however, for the message was always the same curt greeting: "Hello," in sloppy red ketchup script.

Denise wasn't sure what was harder to understand, the paranormal events themselves or Mary's reaction to them. Denise says today: "I had asked Mary why these things didn't bother her, because she and her sister had always acted like it was no big deal. She said, 'They don't bother me because I know it's my mom. Things like this happen at my house all the time.'"

After a while, Mary's hypothesis about the ghost's identity began to make sense. "There was another time," Denise says, "when Mary and her sister had gone to the ICU to see their dad who had just had a stroke. They had just gotten back from the hospital, and we were standing around one of the kitchen counters talking about him, when all at once the knives in one container behind us flew over our heads one by one and buried themselves in the wooden counter we were standing by. That really scared me."

Mary, on the other hand, wasn't fazed in the least. "Mom," she called out into the air, "don't worry, Dad's going to be OK." Denise walked away hoping that the ghost of Mary's mom wasn't going to injure anyone, and things soon went back to normal. Well, normal for Mary's place at least.

The restaurant acquired some fame among the young people in Bailey and those adults who had managed to retain something of their imaginations. "Some of the younger kids would show up with a Ouija board and try to contact the spirit, intent on determining if it really was Mary's mom." Perhaps because of her supernatural experiences at home, Mary was easygoing about this newfound interest in her establishment.

Though the restaurant began to founder financially, Mary continued to do the best job she could with the ghost of her mother hovering over her shoulder, and things continued as usual. All that changed in December 1995 when she was stricken with a brain aneurysm. Denise is convinced that her first contact with Mary's spirit occurred the moment her best friend had passed on: "I was in the hospital with her just before they took her to brain surgery. In the car on the way home, my radio was giving me nothing, the entire bandwidth—nothing but static. Just as I was reaching to turn the radio off, that funeral song came on by Vince Gill, 'Go Rest High on the Mountain.'" When she had got back home, Mary's sister called from the hospital to tell her that Mary had died during the operation.

Denise and Mary had been best friends, and Denise had managed the restaurant pretty well since it opened, so when Mary suddenly died, her family asked Denise if she wanted to buy the place. "I did, and ever since the day I took it over, things began happening at my house and at the restaurant." It seems that Mary was determined to keep her promise to Denise about letting her know if there was anything on the other side.

Denise soon learned that Mary was just as attached to the restaurant as her mother was. The former owner's spirit first got involved with the establishment just before the restaurant was about to undergo an inspection from the Michigan Health Department. Unable to get any sleep on the eve of the inspection that would determine if she could open the restaurant, Denise was tossing and turning through the night. It was sometime past midnight when Mary decided to intervene. "Out of the corner of my bedroom there was a bright light that came up. And all I could hear in my mind was Mary's voice. She was calling me by my nickname, using the same words over and over, 'It'll be okay, Neicey' she said, 'you'll open it. It'll be okay, you'll open it.'" Denise finally fell asleep to the soothing sound of her best friend's voice. The next day she got a call from the Health Department—everything was approved.

While Mary has continued to come to Denise's aid when things aren't going well, she is something of a mischievous ghost that enjoys giving Denise and her family a few frights as well. "It was about five thirty in the morning about a week after I opened the restaurant, and I was the only one in there at that time," Denise relates. "I was standing at the sink filling up the water to start making coffee when I got the strangest sensation that somebody was standing behind me. The feeling kept getting stronger and stronger, and I knew that if I turned around she was going to be standing there. I mean I knew that she would be there; there was absolutely no doubt in my mind. But for some reason I just couldn't turn around, even though I knew that I would see her. So I just spoke out loud; I said 'Mary, please don't scare me.'" No sooner had she voiced this request than the feeling that Mary was standing right behind her immediately vanished, and Denise was alone in the restaurant again.

Denise sensed Mary's presence on several occasions. There were times when Denise was standing behind the grill cooking and actually mistook the looming presence behind her for one of her employees. Irritated, Denise would spin around to tell whomever it was to move, but there would be nobody there. Sometimes Mary's presence was much more prominent. Denise explains: "One day I was standing at the grill with another employee when I was suddenly hit by this almost overpowering perfume. I asked my employee if she was wearing perfume; she told me she wasn't. So I asked her if she could smell that, and she was like, 'smell what?' For a good 15 minutes, wherever I walked in the restaurant, the smell would follow me. I was in the back room when I realized that the smell was Jovan White Musk, which was Mary's favorite perfume when she was alive."

Mary didn't haunt Denise only at the restaurant. "I bought her TV and VCR from her kids," Denise says, "and almost as soon as I moved [the TV] into my house, it would turn off and on and the volume would go up and down by itself." Mary also seemed to like Denise's brand new glider rocker. On more than one night, Denise would be awakened by the sound of the rocker squeaking in the living room. When she made her way down the hall and to the entrance of the room, she would see the chair moving back and forth on its own.

Things got worse in Denise's home in 1997 when financial constraints forced her to close the restaurant. "I think that even though Mary was getting ready to sell the restaurant before she died, when I finally let the place go, it upset her badly," Denise recalls. The bizarre incidents at her home became more frequent. Almost every evening, the rocking chair moved violently; sometimes the entire Hard family would wake up in the middle of the night to the sound of their television's volume on full blast. Denise states that even other employees' homes were visited by Mary's ghost right after the restaurant had closed down and that Mary's family was now coping with the spirits of both Mary and her mother in their household. It seems that the Manning women had a knack for coming back from the dead.

Denise endured Mary's ghost for two more years before she and her family moved down to Florida. Though she believed that she might shake her best friend's spirit with the big location change, Denise's hopes for a peaceful home in a new state faded when it became obvious that Mary had no qualms about moving down to balmy Florida as well. Indeed, there were times when the hauntings grew so bad in their new home that Denise's children were too scared to sleep in their beds at night. Mary only calmed down when Denise and her husband finally asked her as nicely as they could to stop. While things have quieted somewhat in the Hard household since then, Mary still makes her presence known from time to time, particularly if Denise has been talking about her during daylight hours.

Although Mary's ghost has spread a fair degree of fear in Denise's family, she has been responsible for some positive developments as well. While the Hard family has gradually become accustomed to their resident spirit, Denise herself has grown more tuned in to the supernatural world because of it. Back when Denise was working with Mary in the Bailey restaurant, she was petrified of the ghost of Mary's mother. But now with supernatural events being an almost daily occurrence, Denise says that ghosts don't really bother her anymore. Denise's voice gets thoughtful when she considers the effect that Mary has had on her: "I can almost say that Mary's passing has sent me on a spiritual journey. I can...I don't know how to put it...it's almost given me a psychic ability. Now I can sense not just her but other spirits too." Is this heightened sensitivity to the supernatural Mary's last gift to her friend? Or is describing Denise's newfound ability as a "gift" a little bit inaccurate? Whatever the case, Denise still recalls Mary's promise with a smile. "Well, Neicey," Mary had told Denise when she was still alive, "I'll let you know if there's anything there when I get to the other side."

The Michigan Bell Building

Many people who have worked, visited or studied in the Grand Rapids Michigan Bell building have long acknowledged that things are not quite right on the second floor. Some have reported the distinct feeling of being watched as they walked empty hallways—of a presence, malevolent and unseen, that causes the temperature in rooms to plummet, opens and closes doors, plays with light switches and moves ceiling tiles. One employee was walking to the elevator at the end of his workday when he noticed a young woman he had never seen before standing on the stairs. He stopped and was just about to ask her who she was when she vanished into thin air.

Rumor has it that workers in the Michigan Bell building have grown so uncomfortable on the second story that the telephone company has vacated the entire floor. Though no one ever hits the "2" button on the elevator anymore, the lift sometimes stops there anyway. The door opens, and for several tense moments the person on the elevator stares into the darkened hallway before the door closes again. Some witnesses claim to have caught a glimpse of a terror-stricken woman running from an unseen assailant just before the door slides shut. Some have frantically opened the door to assist the woman, only to find the hallway deserted and deadly quiet.

The origin of the tortured spirits that haunt the halls of Michigan Bell's second floor is believed to be buried in the history of Grand Rapids. It is a gruesome story of domestic violence that goes back to 1907, when an ill-fated young couple moved into town from Detroit, hoping to make a new start in the bustling young burg.

The Michigan Bell building is host to many mysterious and eerie events, all seemingly focused on the second floor.

Warren and Virginia Randall rented a house downtown on the corner of Davidson and Fountain Street shortly after arriving in Grand Rapids. While we cannot know what kind of relationship the couple had in Detroit, or even during the first year in their new home, things went tragically wrong after Warren was crippled in a gruesome workplace accident in 1908. Working as a brakeman for the Grand Rapids and Indiana Railroad, the young man was standing in the wrong place when a car derailed; he ended up losing his leg in the ensuing carnage. Things got hellish in the Randall household after that.

Warren could not come to terms with his dependence on his wooden leg. Everywhere he looked, all he saw were the limitations of his sudden handicap, and it was not long before the workings of his mind changed to match the misshapen lurch of his one-legged gait. Virginia Randall received the brunt of his vicious insecurities.

We have no way of knowing whether Virginia grew distant after Warren's accident, but it is quite apparent that he became convinced his young wife was unfaithful. Neighbors reported frightful rows coming from the Randall household as he started giving voice to his jealous neuroses evermore frequently. His roaring accusations were heard down the entire block and soon everyone was whispering about Virginia's trysts with the fruit vendor, with the local butcher…with every man Warren could think of. Things got so bad that on one night, Warren was spotted chasing his wife down the street with a straight razor, threatening to kill her. Virginia finally left Warren early in the month of August 1910.

Who knows what Warren promised Virginia, but he lured her out on the evening of August 26. It was a fine night, and after the couple went on a carriage ride, they ended up back at their old home. What transpired next will forever remain a mystery, but at some point after they had closed the door of their rooming house behind them, Warren must have decided that life was not worth living.

Post-mortem investigations revealed that Warren had clubbed Virginia to death with his wooden leg. He then dragged her into the bedroom, locked the door, stuffed towels in every opening in the room and then unscrewed a gas fixture in the wall, flooding the room with deadly fumes. It seems that death by asphyxiation was not working fast enough for Warren. He slit his own throat with a straight razor before the gas killed him.

Nobody gave any thought to the heavy silence that had descended on the Randall house until about two weeks later, when the neighbors noticed a ghastly stench coming from the place. Members from the Board of Health and the gas company were sent to investigate. Upon opening the front door to the house, all the agents present recoiled in disgust at the combined stench of gas and decay. By the time the police were called in and broke into the couple's old bedroom, both the corpses were blackened by rot. Warren could only be identified by his wooden leg.

No one moved into the house after the discovery in the bedroom. The entire neighborhood was aware of an oppressive foreboding that hung in the air around the place. Stories of bizarre noises coming from within began to circulate only days after the corpses were taken out of the house. Strange cries were heard in the middle of the night and lights were seen flickering on and off. Parents had taken to telling their kids not to play anywhere near the Randall house. It was one of those rare bits of parental advice that children actually take to heart; indeed, the air of evil that hung over the place was so thick that even the most adventurous youths steered clear of it.

Under consistent pressure from nearby residents, the city finally demolished the house in 1920 and for a while at least, the Randall ghosts were quiet. That changed in 1924 when the Michigan Bell Telephone Company bought the empty lot and put up their own building. There have been reports of strange occurrences on the second floor ever since the Michigan Bell building was erected. People have attributed the thumping sounds, moving objects and cold presence to the incident at the Randall house almost from the onset. The young woman seen by some employees, usually at the end of their working day, is assumed to be Virginia Randall. And the phone calls being made from the second floor to Grand Rapids residents in the middle of the night, phone calls of frantic unintelligible whispering abruptly cut off by a disconnecting line—could those, as well, be calls from Virginia, forever reliving the final terrifying moments of her life? Many believe so.

The Ghosts of Pine Cottage

There are a number of historical explanations for the ghostly activity in Pine Cottage on Mackinac Island. Maybe restless Chippewa spirits, upset at being disturbed by the large number of tourists that flock to the island every summer, are responsible for the unexplained sights and sounds that are heard in the building. Or perhaps the souls of dead American and British soldiers—killed by the mortal perforation of musket ball or the crash of cannon—are still bitter at being taken before their time. Could there be restless spirits of mountain men killed in the American wilderness while working for John Jacob Astor's American Fur Company? And of course there was the tragedy that shocked the entire island in 1942, when a woman living in Pine Cottage was found murdered in her room—her assassin slipping away into a rainy summer night, never to be revealed. It could be one, or several, of these spirits that reside in Pine Cottage. Indeed, Mackinac Island's tumultuous history reveals more than enough reason for unsettled souls to remain behind after earthly strife had relegated their bodies to the dust.

It was 11,000 years ago and the Great Lakes themselves were still young when the Chippewa Indians first looked upon the high, forested cliffs of the tiny island. They rowed across the northern waters of Lake Huron and were the first humans to set foot on Mackinac. Most impressed by the island's peculiar limestone formations, the Chippewa took to burying their dead in the caves.

It was not until 1634, when a French-Canadian *coureur de bois* named Jean Nicolet rowed through the Straits of Mackinac, that the Europeans knew Mackinac Island even existed. Throughout the rest of North America's colonial period, the tiny island repeatedly resurfaced as a focal point in the Great Lakes' history.

The British took the island from the French after the French and Indian War and built a fort there in 1780. The Americans acquired Fort Mackinac by treaty with the British after the Revolution, but the British took it back after an amphibious assault in July 1812. They managed to hold onto the fort throughout the War of 1812, until it was ceded to the Americans in an 1815 peace treaty. After the war, the island became the center of operations for Astor's American Fur Company in the Great Lakes region. Innumerable traders came and went with the seasons, rowing deep into the woods to trap their furs and establish relations with the Indians during the winter months. Come spring and summer, the island was the fur terminus of the northern United States, and those men who survived the treacherous work season came back to Mackinac Island loaded with their bounty.

Bob Hughey was not too concerned about the island's turbulent history when he bought Pine Cottage from the Moral Rearmament Organization in 1962. An enterprising restaurateur, Hughey's main interests were dollars and cents. Though he was warned that the house was haunted when he bought it, more immediate monetary ambitions eclipsed any supernatural concerns he may have entertained.

Located on steeply rising Bogan Lane a mere 2 blocks from the shores of Lake Huron, the centennial home is enormous, with a northern wing, a wraparound front porch, 3 floors and 42 rooms. Bob was intent on making

Pine Cottage into a thriving restaurant during Mackinac's bustling summer months, but it was not long after he purchased the building that he realized he had something much more than a mere business venture on his hands.

It happened one night early in the spring of 1962. Bob was up late playing cards with his sister-in-law Becky, his brother Joe and one of his cooks. Their lively chatter was interrupted by the sound of the front door creaking open. A second later, everybody at the table simultaneously jumped when the same door slammed shut. In the next moment, someone's heavy footfalls were clomping up the stairs.

"Bob?" Joe broke the silence. "I think somebody came in."

"You don't say, Joe," his brother snorted. "Just wait here; I'll go take a look."

Bob ended up searching the entire house, but there was no trace of anyone. It was then that he recalled the warnings from the previous owners that the place was haunted. Yet even if he was the type of person who would leave because of some inexplicable noises, the weight of all the new responsibilities that came with setting up his new business did not allow for such an option.

It was the following day and Bob Hughey had just gotten off the telephone with his wife, Pat, when he had a much more dramatic encounter with one of Pine Cottage's spirits. Pat was back in Scottsdale, Arizona, waiting for the kids to finish their final exams before coming up to Michigan with the whole family for the summer. Bob had just been telling her about the previous night's incident, but she was much more interested in making sure that Bob picked out the bedroom with the biggest closet for her.

He was looking around the house for a nice closet for Pat, and had just walked into Room Four on the first floor when a woman he had never seen before burst out of the closet. Her hair was piled into a bun on top of her head, her eyes were glowing red, and there was nothing but empty space where her legs should have been. The top half of this woman came tearing into the room, obviously frenzied with fear and confusion. She flew right by Bob, practically knocking him over in her rush to get out of the room, and quickly disappeared out the window. After a headlong sprint took him out of the building and a few blocks down the street, Hughey stood there shaking in fear and exhaustion. If there was ever a moment when he might have abandoned Pine Cottage, that probably would have been it…but he stayed on. Did Bob's decision to stay after this encounter make him an exceptional man?

Who knows? It was only 1962 after all, and no one had seen *The Shining* or *Poltergeist* yet—perhaps Hollywood had not yet instilled the fear of the nether-world into Bob Hughey. Or more likely, the threat of the unknown was insufficient to dampen the enthusiasm of the entrepreneur, and come ghosts or goblins, Bob intended to follow through with his plans to open up his restaurant.

Nevertheless, Pat and the Hugheys' five children had a much easier time dealing with the ghosts in Pine Cottage over the years than Bob did. He was less than thrilled at the idea that the legless lady might appear again, scaring the wits out of patrons, employees or his kids. While the floating apparition that Bob encountered in the spring of 1962 was never reported by anyone again, as time passed it became evident that there was more than one restless spirit in Pine Cottage.

Pat was legally blind and so was spared any ghost sightings during the years she lived in the house, but she would hear footsteps late in the night when everyone was asleep and often sensed an ominous other presence when she was supposed to be alone. There were times when she was lounging in the tub and could have sworn that something was in the bathroom with her, standing just beyond her limited field of vision, watching silently. Or on some evenings, just as she was settling into bed, her room would suddenly grow cold, and Chipper, the family dog, would bolt off the bed and run to the corner of the room, growling at some invisible presence.

The number of supernatural encounters in Pine Cottage increased dramatically after the restaurant was opened to the public. Anyone who spent any time in the building was likely to have some kind of paranormal experience. The five Hughey children often ran to their parents' room in the middle of the night, complaining that someone was trying to push them out of their beds. When the Hugheys made Pine Cottage into a bed and breakfast, many guests claimed they saw something big and white dash across their window before suddenly disappearing into nothingness. And then there were the numerous reports about rooms that suddenly grew cold on balmy summer evenings.

One morning at the breakfast table, Darwin, one of Bob and Pat's children, was looking puzzled at his grandmother, who was visiting the family for a few months. "Grandma," he finally asked, "why were you standing by my bed last night?"

Pat's mother initially dismissed the question as a product of her grandson's active imagination. "But I wasn't in your room last night, dear."

"Grandma," Darwin responded with childish exasperation, "Yes you were. You were wearing a long white dress." The resolve in her grandson's voice made her look up from her bacon and eggs. She suddenly remembered all the supernatural stories and decided to play along, lest Darwin get too frightened. "I just came in to cover you up," she said. While this satisfied the young boy's curiosity, from that day on Pat's mother always felt a little bit uneasy in Pine Cottage.

Of all the kinds of ghostly run-ins, the single most common encounter was with a little girl with long blonde hair and big, tear-filled eyes. It was late one morning, and Bob and Pat's daughter, Yvonne, was just getting dressed to work in the restaurant when she heard timid sobbing just outside her door. Assuming one of her siblings was aggrieved over some childish wrong, she opened her door to find a young girl she had never seen before. The little girl had blonde hair and was dressed in white. When Yvonne moved forward to comfort her, she bolted down the hall and around the corner. Yvonne tried to follow her but saw only an empty hall when she rounded the corner just behind the little apparition. The child was seen on numerous other occasions. Sometimes she ran from consoling adults, and other times she would simply vanish before their eyes. Bob Hughey lost one of his more dedicated cooks because of this little ghost's disappearing act. The man had just come out of the shower when he saw the girl standing in front of him, gently crying into her cupped hands. He asked her what was wrong, to which she replied,

"Mommy, I want to go home." When he reached forward to comfort her, she just evaporated into the air, leaving no trace of ever having been there.

When Pat asked a neighbor if a blonde girl had ever lived in Pine Cottage, she was told a sad story about a family that used to summer in Mackinac Island many years ago. Two young parents would come in from Detroit with their daughter for July and August every year. The mother and father enjoyed partying, and were out drinking most of the time, leaving the girl alone. People walking by could hear her sobbing late into the night. Pat's neighbor had heard that the girl had died one fall soon after the family moved back to Detroit. She had long, straight blonde hair, big blue eyes, and was often seen in a white dress.

But not all of the haunts in Pine Cottage were so wide-eyed. It was on a frigid winter night in Mackinac, and Bob was sent to the cold bedroom in the basement after he had gotten into a fight with his wife. If Pat had any regrets about the quarrel, at least she would get the bed to herself for the next few nights. She was sure that it would take Bob a couple of days before he swallowed his pride and offered anything resembling an apology. So she was surprised when he appeared at her bedside the same night they had argued, timidly asking if he could sleep with her. Pat laughed. "Why?" was her haughty response. Her husband did not say a word, but crawled into the bed beside her and fell into a restless sleep.

The next morning he explained that he had been woken by someone pulling on his covers. Groggy at first, he was sure he was partly dreaming and casually tugged back at his blankets, trying to get under them and get back to sleep.

But whatever was at the end of his bed responded by yanking even harder, almost dragging Bob off his mattress and onto the floor. In the next moment he was wide awake, involved in a fierce tug-of-war with an unknown opponent, cursing the ghosts he had gotten so used to in Pine Cottage. His anger turned to sheer horror when he finally opened his eyes to see what he had assumed would be an invisible opponent. There, at the foot of his bed, he saw something that looked like a man hunched over on its hands and knees, pulling at his blankets with what he swore was a grin on its misshapen face. A row of horn-like protrusions grew down the middle of its back. He was so scared that he remembers nothing of his dash to Pat's bed.

The hauntings continued for as long as the Hugheys owned the place, and no single satisfactory explanation was offered as to why the building was so full of phantoms. The lonely summers for the little girl from Detroit explain her apparition, and the murder in 1942 may account for the disembodied woman who rushed at Bob when he first bought the house. However, a significant number of other people have experienced countless, seemingly unrelated, incidents. The Hugheys sold their business on Mackinac Island in 1995 and moved to St. Ignace to start up another restaurant. So far, there have been no reports of ghosts from the new owners of Pine Cottage.

The Haunted Manor

White House Manor was built in 1929, a gift from Charles Rogers for Harriet Thornton, his wife-to-be. Considering the sheer opulence of the place, it seems that Charles felt just fine giving his emotions material expression. Located on Nine Mile Road in Novi, a western suburb of Detroit, Rogers' stately declaration of love for his fiancée still stands today, an impressive architectural creation that spares nothing when it comes to luxury. The house appears to have been built with an amalgamation of New England and Old South influences. Lofty columns, elaborate balconies, pediments and embossed cornices speak volumes of the care that went into the design. The interior is no less impressive; much of the woodwork is hand-carved, thick trimming surrounds the floors and ceilings, and vibrant stained glass windows add rich color to the classic beauty inside.

But the most outstanding feature of the house is in the entrance hall, where an enormous staircase with cherry wood banisters sweeps down from the second floor. It is an elegantly curving structure that is offset by the strict linear patterns dominating the rest of the room. Legend has it that Charles Rogers had this stairway built to satisfy one specific dream he had entertained ever since love's first glance had fallen on Harriet. From that day on, Charles had an image of walking their future daughter down just such a staircase to a resplendent hall, and into the arms of her future husband. While such a dream may not be the typical vision of a man who has just glimpsed his true love for the first time, the immense wealth of the Rogers family was well able to support such idiosyncrasies. And so that castle in the air was made into a wooden staircase; and if Charles' busy schedule did not allow him to obsess about the tentative wedding march, it is safe to say that it was almost always in the back of his head.

Harriet, of course, cannot be blamed any more than Charles can for the four boys she gave birth to. Years passed, and try as they might, the couple had no luck conceiving another child. There would be no Rogers girl for Charles and Harriet. Charles would never live out the vision that had moved him to have the stairway built. He took the realization the way people greet the major disappointments of their lives. But as his sons grew and got married, a new idea began to worm its way into his head: what about a granddaughter? Perhaps he would live long enough to walk a granddaughter down the stairwell. Perhaps.

A few more decades passed before Charles was close to living out his slightly modified lifelong dream. For his eldest granddaughter was getting married, and her father was fine with having Charles give her away. The Rogers prepared their home with nearly fanatical zeal. White House Manor was completely redecorated; mantles, doorways, walls and staircases were adorned with every kind of flower imaginable, a veritable army of chefs was hired to prepare a banquet of Dionysian proportions, and a flotilla of invitations was sent out.

But then the unspeakable occurred. With the kind of tactlessness typical of many young people, the couple eloped the very night before their planned ceremony. The day of the wedding found an old Charles Rogers alone in the entrance hall, staring up in despair at the staircase he loved so much. It is said that he was never the same after that, and he passed away soon after, dying of a broken heart on November 11, 1942.

His body was laid in state at the foot of those same stairs that had been such a huge disappointment when he was alive. Harriet lived in the house for a few years longer until she too passed away. Her casket was placed in the library before it was buried next to her husband's plot.

Though Charles and Harriet were dead, subsequent owners of White House Manor would certainly agree that the building still belonged to them. The first record of bizarre activity comes from the first family to own the place after the Rogers. Published paranormal expert Marion Kuclo heard the story when she was lecturing to a group of women about hauntings one night in 1983. After the show one of her audience members, an old woman named Arlene, told her about an experience she had at the White House Manor in the 1940s when she was a young girl. Arlene was best friends with Mary Ellen Crusoe, whose parents bought the elegant house after Harriet Rogers had passed on.

The two girls were sitting in the mansion's library one day when their quiet talk was interrupted by the loud crash of shattering glass. Startled almost out of their socks, Arlene and Mary Ellen looked to see that the glass covering for one of the paintings mounted on the north wall had just fallen off on its own and now lay shattered. The butler came running in moments later and was outraged at the sight of the broken glass strewn all over the floor. The angry man didn't spare any of his thoughts on the girls, who tearfully protested their innocence. In the following argument, no one even thought to consider that the body of Harriet Rogers, before it was buried, was laid in this room and that her casket had rested against the north wall.

Arlene's bizarre experiences in White House Manor did not end with shattered glass in the library. She and her friend were also accused of opening doors and slamming them shut, turning lights on and off, and even hiding under the stairs in the cellar and making strange noises. After Kuclo had heard Arlene's account of what went on in White House Manor so many years ago, she went to take a look at the place for herself. She was not disappointed in her findings.

When Kuclo visited the manor in 1983 it had been converted into a restaurant. Two Italian men, the Cervi brothers, had bought the house in 1981 and changed it into a fine dining establishment. Yet while Charles and Harriet Rogers could no longer enjoy good food, they apparently did not think this was enough reason to leave their old home. Indeed, it seems that human awareness of their phantom presence became their own food and drink. Almost everyone who frequented the restaurant regularly, from managers to employees to patrons, had some sort of experience with the spirits of the two original inhabitants.

One location of frequent strange activities was the ladies room on the second floor. When women were in there by themselves, they often heard footsteps, knocking on the walls, and sometimes the toilets in unoccupied stalls would flush on their own. The bathroom used to be connected to the master bedroom, and though we'd like to think that the spirit in the ladies' room would belong to Harriet Rogers, there is reason to believe that the mischievous ghost of Charles Rogers might be having a bit too much fun in the afterlife.

Sherry, the bartender in the restaurant, had a few hair-raising experiences with what she was assumed was a male ghost. She was climbing the main stairs one night after the restaurant was closed when she felt something brush by her. Sherry froze where she stood and spun around, only to see the empty entrance hall down below. Thoroughly spooked, she turned to resume her walk up the stairs when she felt someone pinch her. As she sprinted in fear up the rest of the stairs, she heard a man chuckling in her ear.

If the ghost of Charles Rogers is something of a flirt, it might be said that his wife Harriet is a temperance advocate. Sherry had been scared out of her skin more than once when the huge mirror hanging behind the bar would shatter for no apparent reason. At other times entire racks of wineglasses would seemingly acquire volition and leap off the bar onto the floor—sending a deafening crash throughout the house. Upon hearing Sherry's accounts, Marion Kuclo did a little bit of research and found that the bar was where the old library used to be. The wall where the mirror was hung was the same wall that Harriet Rogers's casket had been set beside before she was buried; it was the same place that had gotten Arlene and Mary Ellen in trouble so many years ago.

Another employee, a waiter by the name of Richard Shank, was about to throw back a rye and coke he had made for himself after a busy shift when he was hit by the overwhelming feeling that somebody was standing right beside him. A strong, almost overwhelming odor of lavender perfume mingled there with a barely restrained hostility. For no apparent reason at all, adrenaline raced through Richard's veins, as if he was about to fight an invisible opponent. In the next moment, he heard a woman shout "No!" and the glass was slapped from his hand. He would never take another drink at work again.

Mike Cervi, who owned half the business and was head manager, had more than one spooky incident in the mansion. "I loved the place," Mike recalls, "but so many things went on that were just too damn strange." Mike became acquainted with the ghosts in White House Manor late at night long after the restaurant had closed for the evening. "I'd be the only one in the restaurant—straightening out the paperwork, counting the money—when these noises would start up; it was like there was somebody else in the building. There were footsteps walking up and down the main stairs, doors would open and close. On some nights, after I'd shut off all the lights and locked up, I'd be halfway to my car before one of the lights would flick on again. It was downright spooky, 'cause I knew that there was no one in there; the lights would just go on by themselves."

It was not an abundance of ghosts, but a shortage of greenbacks, which impelled the Cervi brothers to close down the restaurant in 1984. The place was deserted until 1987, when Suzi Romanik and her brother, Steve, opened another restaurant. By now everyone in the area knew that the building was haunted and the Romaniks were warned about the Rogers ghosts. Maybe the two new proprietors thought they could exorcise the ghosts from the place with extreme changes: they renamed the mansion "Home Sweet Home" and ordered radical renovations, replacing the classic décor with an eclectic bohemian design. Yet it soon became obvious that the ghostly couple was not at all deterred by the new look.

The ghosts continued as before, and things reached a head one evening in October 1998 when the Romaniks gave Marion Kuclo permission to lead a séance in the mansion after the restaurant was closed. Several of the participants went into strange trances and one of the women passed out as the chandelier on the ceiling above Kuclo's party began to shake violently. There was a loud racket upstairs and it seemed like the whole house was shaking under thundering footfalls and the sounds of heavy items being thrown about on the second floor. But when some of the group ran upstairs to take a look, not a single item of furniture was disturbed from where it was placed. But despite all the chaos, Kuclo maintained that nobody at the séance had spoken to either Charles or Harriet Rogers.

Though that night in October marked the peak of paranormal activity in the household, the bizarre day-to-day events continued to haunt the Romaniks' establishment until they finally closed the restaurant down. Another restaurant called Shiro has opened up in the old White House Manor. As of yet, no stories have emerged from the new business.

The Calumet Theatre

Actress Adysse Lane was standing horrorstruck before the sold-out crowd at the Calumet Theatre, unable to recall her next line. Staring out into the darkness beyond the stage, she posed dramatically, buying herself some time to snap back into the script, but nothing came; the leading lady could not remember the words that her character, Katharina, spoke to end the play. Just as she was about to lose herself to panic, she felt a strong, gentle force slowly lift her arms upward to the Calumet Theatre's second balcony. Her eyes followed, and from out of the darkness above, a striking female apparition suddenly appeared. Ms. Lane later remembered how atypically beautiful the woman hovering there before her was, with "dark eyes and a pale complexion" crowned by a dark shock of short, curly hair.

It was the summer of 1958, and William Shakespeare's *The Taming of the Shrew* was being performed at the old theater in the Upper Peninsula town of Calumet. The theater was constructed in 1900, when the copper on the Keweenaw Peninsula was making men rich, and Calumet's elite hoped to plant the seeds of higher culture into the rough town. So was born the extravagant Calumet Theatre, as opulent as any of metropolitan America's playhouses. Gilded decorations arched over a thick velvet curtain and ornate stage, which was fronted by row upon row of plush seats. During its heyday, the opera house stood as the town's sole Tower of Song and was host to the stars of the American stage, including such 20th-century dramatic luminaries as Sarah Bernhardt, Leslie Carter, Houdini and Madame Helena Modjeska.

Adysse Lane did not realize she was staring a part of the theater's history in the face the night she was stranded deep in *The Taming of the Shrew*'s fifth act with no hope of finishing the play gracefully. The woman hovering high above her in the darkness was the same woman whose portrait hung in the theater's lobby: none other than Helena Modjeska herself. Ms. Lane was lucky, for on that night, the spirit of the legendary thespian seemed intent on playing patron saint of distressed performers. As Adysse Lane stared up at the ghostly figure, Madame Modjeska's mouth slowly began to move, somehow whispering the opening lines to Katharina's last speech in the Shakespeare play:

> Fie, fie! unknit that threatening unkind brow,
> And dart not scornful glances from those eyes,
> To wound thy lord, thy king, thy governor:
> It blots thy beauty as frosts do bite the meads…

These first four lines triggered the rest of the speech in Adysse's memory, and in the next moment, she found the oft-rehearsed words spilling from her mouth, even as the old actress above recited them. The play's last speech rang through the theater and the show ended amid thunderous applause. Ms. Lane poked her head through the curtain and looked up to see if the apparition was still there. The house lights were on, and Adysse Lane could see that the members of the appreciative audience on the second balcony were up on their feet, clapping…but there was no sign at all of the mysterious woman who had saved her from complete humiliation.

Ms. Lane realized the woman's identity later on that night when she was socializing with some of the audience members in the lobby. There on the wall hung the portrait of the famous Helena Modjeska, whose painted eyes stared at the actress with an eerie kind of knowing. It was then that it dawned on her what had happened: that the spirit of Helena Modjeska had come to the aid of another actress in her time of need.

Since that night in 1958, there have been frequent reports of bizarre incidents at the Calumet Theatre. There are stories of a female apparition drifting over the catwalks above the stage, wandering the dark, cramped hallway that runs down the back of the second balcony and fretting over her appearance in the building's dressing room. By all accounts, this figure bears a striking resemblance to the portrait in the theater's lobby. For whatever reason, it seems that Helena Modjeska has developed an attachment to the Calumet Theatre in the afterlife.

Why Madame Modjeska would pick the opera house in Calumet is anyone's guess. She was a 19th-century superstar after all, a cosmopolitan celebrity renowned throughout the United States for her memorable portrayals of Shakespearean characters and received as royalty in New York, Philadelphia, Los Angeles or London. Some might think it strange that she would choose a theater in out-of-the-way Calumet as her ultimate resting place. Not that the town theater wasn't a spectacular building, or Calumet itself wasn't worthy of her presence, but Madame Modjeska's home was in California, and if she really had to haunt a place, why not the Metropolitan Opera in New York? Or the famous Chestnut Street Theatre in Philadelphia? She had performed in these

Helena Modjeska apparently appeared to rescue an actress who had forgotten her lines.

prestigious venues as well. What was it about the Calumet Theatre in the modest Upper Peninsula town that drew the attention of this star of the stage?

There has been some speculation that it was Adysse Lane's part in *The Taming of the Shrew* that got Helena's attention. Indeed, it's been said that the legendary actress always connected emotionally with the character of Katharina and though she was always looking for an opportunity to take on the role, none of the prominent theater groups performed the play while she was alive. Perhaps Helena's ghost was just another audience member in the Calumet Theatre that night and took it on herself to help out Adysse when she began to flounder.

It looks as if Helena has taken a special liking to the lavish old opera house, for things have never been quite the same in the building since Adysse Lane was assisted with Katharina's last words on that fateful night. Along with the numerous sightings of the curly-haired apparition, employees working late have heard loud crashes in the middle of the night; lights are known to go on and off by themselves; and on more than one occasion, the first workers arriving in the morning reported the stage curtains they had left closed the night before hanging wide open.

Meanwhile, people claim to have experienced odd feelings around Helena Modjeska's portrait—twitching nervously under the watchful eyes of the actress in the 19th-century painting. Many have sworn that something in the painting was actually watching them. And it seems that the frequency of strange events increases when this same portrait is temporarily taken down. It is then, almost invariably, that reports of being closely watched by an invisible spectator rise dramatically. Patron and employee alike have often had to leave the building because of a strong sense that they were being studied by a highly critical, disapproving, presence.

Whether she is assisting frightened actresses or keeping a close eye on everyone in the old theater, it seems that Madame Modjeska has become the Calumet Theatre's supernatural matriarch. Until, perhaps, some other old opera house puts on *The Taming of the Shrew.*

Chapter 4

Haunted Houses

★ ★ ★

More than any other worldly possessions people claim as their own,
no objects reflect individuals' personalities like the homes they live in.
Tidy or messy, modest or extravagant, houses are not only measures
of people's means and living habits, they are also the havens that
individuals construct against the large outside world—small islands of
individuality amid the vast impersonal ocean that is the public
space. Our homes are ours, containing all the objects, effects
and energies that are distinct to who we are.

It is no wonder, then, that people talk of houses having "personalities,"
or that some places seem to retain an intangible energy, stemming from a
sense of what the abode used to be, from the lives of its former inhabi-
tants. And then there are those houses that are afflicted by something
more than intangible energies. Usually, these are domiciles distressed
by some dramatic event in the past, buildings brought to life by spirits
either unwilling or unable to move on after they themselves have ceased.
Despite deeds of ownership and the wishes of living inhabitants, the
ghosts that drift through these haunted houses usually don't seem to be
too concerned with the effect they have on the other, corporeal, dwellers
in the household. And while so many of us are fascinated by stories of
such possessed manors, haunted houses are still places we would prefer to
hear about rather than experience. Following are a number of reports—
observed from a safe distance—of people's own
experiences with ghosts in their homes.

A Ghostly Guest

If any homes in historic Bay City fit the stereotypical haunted house profile, it would be those prestigious establishments located in the city's former "lumber baron" part of town. This area is roughly a mile-long stretch of stately Victorian homes arrayed along Center Avenue just east of the city's old downtown area. The strip was created in the late 19th century, when Bay City was a major center of operations for Michigan's booming lumber industry. Those aggressive entrepreneurs who got richest off the lumber trade exhibited their wealth with the massive homes they constructed here. Each house that was built was an attempt to outdo the one that came just before it, and for the present-day spectator, the spectacular row of ostentatious establishments growing evermore grand as the avenue goes on stands as a splendid display of human avarice at its best.

In his book *Haunted Michigan: Recent Encounters With Active Spirits,* Reverend Gerald S. Hunter reports on the peculiar events that took place in one of these opulent abodes which is as haunted as it looks. "Rick and Joan Hemphill" are pseudonyms Hunter gives to the couple that finally got their wish when they moved into one of the big houses on Center Avenue. Joan first learned of the spirit in her house when she and her husband were having some of the neighbors over for their housewarming. One of the guests helping Joan take the dishes into the kitchen startled the new homeowner with the oddest question. "So," the woman asked, trying her best to disguise the nervousness in her voice, "have you seen the ghost yet?"

Joan looked her obviously uncomfortable guest in the face before she smiled. "Not yet," she replied, and then changed the subject.

Joan probably would have quickly forgotten the short exchange if it weren't for the strange incidents that began taking place over the next few weeks. Rick, who often came home before his wife or kids, claimed that he would hear what he swore were startled footsteps dashing up the stairs when he turned the key to the front door. Quickly opening the door and running to the second floor to confront the intruder himself, he was greeted with an empty hall every time. On more than one occasion, Joan would notice that the stoppers to her perfume decanters had been removed and were lying by their bottles. The smell of perfume was strong in the air as if someone had been sampling the perfumes. There were a few times when she would come home for lunch to find her children's toys strewn across the parlor floor, but no kids were around to have made the mess.

Rick and Joan decided not to say anything so as to keep the kids from getting scared, but before long the children themselves took notice of the strange occurrences in the house. They complained that someone was taking toys from their rooms, and on some nights, the lights in their bedroom closets turned on and off by themselves. Their parents tried their best, as good, rationally minded adults do, to offer logical explanations for these events. Yet whatever bubble of sensibility Rick and Joan managed to put up around the inexplicable events that were taking place in their new home popped a few days before Christmas in 1998.

The family was gathered in the living room, enjoying the peace of a rare night with no plans. The fireplace was lit, everyone had a mug of hot chocolate, and they were about halfway through Dr. Seuss's *The Grinch Who Stole Christmas* on TV. Joan's five-year-old, Christie, had been getting restless in her mother's lap, repeatedly stretching her neck to look at the large stairway off the front door. Joan was doing her best to ignore her until Christie finally leaned back and whispered into her mother's ear. "Mommy, who's that little girl on the stairs?"

Fear leapt into Joan's throat as she looked through the parlor door to the curving walnut stairway. There, on the first landing, sat a tiny little girl with long blonde hair and wearing a white nightgown. Her legs were curled under her as she sat watching the television from a distance. When Joan turned to look at her, the girl smiled. Trying not to panic, Joan told her daughter that the figure was just a little girl who liked their house and loved their family and just wanted to share some of her Christmas with them. "Maybe it was because Christie was so young that she bought my explanation—thank God," Joan later told Reverend Hunter in an interview.

The child in white remained on the landing until all the Christmas specials were over and vanished the moment the television was turned off. It turns out that Joan did not have to explain to Rick what she had seen after the kids were put to bed, because he had seen the little girl on the landing as well. Over the next few weeks, Rick and Joan would be wakened in the middle of the night by the sound of the television in the parlor. Getting up to investigate, the couple would always stop at the top of the stairs, gaping down at the first landing where the little girl sat, enthralled by the images on the television screen. A few seconds would pass before the girl would look over her shoulder, smile at the two and vanish into thin air, leaving either one of the spooked couple to go downstairs and turn the television off.

The same incident repeated itself for the rest of the winter and into the early spring before the Hemphills decided to invite paranormal enthusiast Reverend Gerald Hunter into their home. One night in mid-spring 1999 the Reverend himself witnessed the same supernatural encounter that had been replaying itself for Joan and Rick since the holidays.

He was lounging in the Hemphills' living room, enjoying a glass of single-malt scotch with his hosts, when the television came on in the adjoining parlor. Their hearts pounded with anticipation as the trio made their way into the blue-lit room where the television buzzed quietly. All three of them peeked around the parlor doorway, and there, sitting on the first landing, was the mysterious little girl in the white nightgown, staring at the flashing television screen with grave interest. But she only stayed for a few more seconds. Noticing the three wonder-struck adults gawking at her from behind the wall, the apparition looked straight at them and smiled sweetly before vanishing completely. Reverend Hunter was so moved by the experience that he wrote the story of the little ghost on Center Avenue in his book the following year.

As for Mr. and Mrs. "Hemphill," they have since gotten used to their ghostly resident, and even their children have become acquainted with the blonde girl who likes to sit on the landing and watch TV. The Hemphills always inform any guests of their spectral boarder, and while some friends and relatives no longer feel comfortable staying in their home, there are others who are fascinated by the blonde waif. Joan herself summed up the new living arrangements in a conversation with Reverend Hunter, saying, "We've come to accept her, and she seems happy with us." And so it is that one family on Center Avenue has taken a little ghost into their fold.

Usher of the Afterlife

In his book *Haunted Michigan,* Reverend Gerald Hunter describes Walter Hunnicut (a pseudonym) as a modest, spiritual man, not given to drama or affectation. Yet whoever said "still waters run deep" had a point with this quiet, unassuming individual who rarely speaks of his string of extraordinary supernatural encounters that began in the fall of 1998.

It was well after the sun had set over the city of Big Rapids, and the lights were out in practically every home on Hutchinson Street. Walter Hunnicut's house was no exception. Every room was draped in the utter stillness of the early morning hours; Walter himself was buried deep under the covers, nestled in bed with his wife, Tara—lost in a dreamless slumber. He usually slept easily through the whole night and so was surprised when a gradual return to consciousness left him wide awake well before his alarm was set to go off. Staring up at the ceiling of his bedroom, he instantly knew that something wasn't right.

Raising his head, Walter saw an old woman with white hair lying in a hospital bed on the other side of his room.

Walter and Tara did not have another bed in their room, nor were they keeping any guests, so one would think that the sight of this uninvited visitor in the middle of the night would surprise the man at the very least. But for some reason, he felt completely calm.

He blinked twice, but she was still there, looking at him with wide-eyed fear. A moment later, he realized the woman's thoughts were in his mind, that she was somehow communicating with him telepathically. "She communicated to me that she had just died," Walter told Reverend Hunter, "and she was wondering if it was all right to move on to the next world. She was frightened, like she didn't know what to do. As she conveyed all this to me, she also told me she was the mother of one of the guys I worked for."

Though he had never seen the woman before, Walter's heart went out to the old lady. Recognizing the fundamental plight of humanity in the woman's last mortal fear, he felt an overwhelming empathy for her. He wanted to reassure her that she was not alone, that everything was going to be fine. No sooner had these thoughts come to him than he knew she had heard them, and her image slowly began to fade away. He saw the hard edge of fear leave her eyes just before she disappeared completely…and he was suddenly alone with his wife again. Walter shook Tara as soon as the old woman was gone. Thrilled at what had just transpired, he told her everything. She listened as best as can be expected of anyone woken at that hour. Silent for a few moments after her husband was finished, Tara reassured Walter that she believed him and went back to sleep. Hunnicut was left awake, uncertain of whether his wife was taking him seriously.

The next morning at work, when Walter learned that his boss's mother had passed away in East Lansing, he knew that she was the woman who had visited him the night before. He brought it up with one of his co-workers at lunch, but the man looked at him as if he had just slipped off the proverbial rocker. Hunnicut then determined that it was probably best to keep these kinds of thoughts to himself.

And there would be more food for such thought before long. Christmas was only a few days away when Walter received his second late-night visitor that year. "Sometime around 2 AM, I drifted awake again," Hunnicut told Hunter, "and this time there was a woman sort of hovering over my bed. She was about 70 years old, with dyed brown hair, wearing a heavy, very modest nightgown. This time, it was someone I had seen before, and I knew instantly she was a friend of my mother's from down in Grand Rapids."

Her approach to communicating with Walter was different from the one the first lady had used, but her message was the same: she had just died and was frightened of moving on. As the spirit of the woman spoke with him, Walter realized that they had been suddenly transported to her house. He had never been at her place before and as he drifted through the kitchen by the side of the dead woman's spirit, he could not help noticing the smallest details of her worldly possessions—the cheap dinette set, the magnets on the fridge, the kitschy ceramic chickens on the shelf above her sink. The two hovered up the stairs and into the woman's bedroom, where they stood at her bedside and looked down at her dead body lying there under her covers.

Her spirit form looked at Walter again; she was frightened. He felt that same sort of compassion for her as he had for the woman who appeared to him in the fall, and he reassured her that everything was OK. The instant that she vanished, he found himself wide awake back in his bed in Big Rapids. Again, he woke up Tara, and this time the couple jotted down the details of the encounter, hoping that they might be able to substantiate the whole encounter with hard facts.

Hunnicut had previously promised his mother that he would go down to Grand Rapids to visit her the next day. There was a lump of apprehension in his throat the entire way down Highway 131, for the woman who had visited him the night before was his mother's next-door neighbor. Breakfast turned to lunch, and Walter was only half conscious of his conversation with his mother, so fixated was he on what was, or wasn't, happening in the house next door. No word came until just before noon, when their talk was interrupted by a knock at his mother's back door.

The neighbor's eldest son was at the doorway. He told Mrs. Hunnicut that he had come to his mother's house to visit her that morning, only to find that she had passed away sometime the night before. Understandably grief-stricken, he asked if the Hunnicuts would mind waiting with him at his mother's place for the coroner to arrive. Walter's heart was beating rapidly in his chest.

His legs trembled when he walked into the old woman's home. Everything there was as he had seen it the night before. The furniture, the fridge magnets, the dinette set, the chickens. When he and his mother went up to take a look at the dead woman in her bedroom, she was lying in the exact same pose that Walter had seen her the night before. It was then that he and his wife knew beyond any doubt that his dreams really were visits from the dead.

But contrary to what the reader may think, Walter was not at all perturbed by this supernatural correspondence. In fact, something about the spiritual visits imbued him with a newfound peace and strengthened his religious faith. He felt privileged that these spirits had chosen him to unburden their worst fears upon. And so his life went on as normal and he kept his two paranormal experiences to himself.

Almost a year went by before Walter would have another ghostly experience. It happened on a mid-October evening in 1999. Walter woke up in the middle of the night to find himself standing in a rest home at his Uncle Larry's bedside. Larry was something of a pariah in Walter's family. A hedonist who had not troubled himself with the consequences of his actions or the feelings of others throughout much of his life, he had spent the bulk of his days womanizing and guzzling booze. He left a long trail of hurt and bitterness behind him, but the person he'd hurt the most was his loving wife.

Looking down at his uncle's still form, he knew that the man was nearing his end. His liver and kidneys were barely functioning as a result of all the alcohol he had consumed, and the lines in his haggard face spoke of a man with nothing left to give. But he was still alive. Walter sensed his uncle's thoughts underneath his closed eyelids. Larry knew that his nephew was a spiritual man, and he had a request for him. Walter knew what it was. He leaned down close to his old uncle's face; "Do you want me to pray with you?" Walter asked. The second the words left his mouth, Larry's eyes shot open and he threw his hands up, grabbing Walter around the neck and pulling the young man down towards him. An instant later, Walter was back in his darkened home, sitting up in bed.

Given his last two experiences with spirits, Walter knew that he had to go see his uncle as soon as possible. Unlike the other two frightened souls, he sensed that his uncle was not dead yet but was terrified at the possibility of dying without absolution for his dissolute and self-centered ways. After work the next day, Walter headed south for Grand Rapids to see Uncle Larry.

Arriving at the nursing home, Walter recognized his uncle's room immediately; it was exactly as it had appeared in his journey the night before. Almost instinctively, he walked up to his uncle's bed and asked the same question he had asked the last time he was there. "Uncle Larry," Walter whispered, "would you like me to pray with you?"

Again, the old man's eyes shot open and he grabbed his nephew, pulling him close. Walter would later say that he had never seen anyone look so scared. They sat together and prayed for a couple of hours before Larry drifted off into a deep sleep. Hunnicut drove back to Big Rapids that night and waited for the call. At around 11 o'clock the next morning, his aunt was on the telephone, telling him that Larry had died in his sleep that morning.

Who knows why some spirits of the recently deceased have chosen Walter to speak to in their final hours? Have the man's actions inadvertently turned him into some kind of gatekeeper to the netherworld? Or perhaps he has been endowed with an innate spiritual sensitivity that attracts lost souls? And why do only some souls come to him, while the vast majority of those people he has known in the Big Rapids area do not? Walter himself is at a loss to explain the purpose behind his encounters. But he does remain grateful for the opportunity to have such eye-opening experiences, and he feels that the contact he has had with these souls before they've departed from the earthly plane is nothing less than a blessing from God.

The Ghost of Mr. Enoch

The year was 1984, and 16-year-old Sherri McElhaney's mind began to race through preparations when her parents announced that they intended to move to a remote house on the outskirts of Battle Creek. Sherri was a lifelong ballet enthusiast and her main concern at the time was ensuring that all the dancing paraphernalia adorning the walls and shelves of her old room would survive the move without a tear, scratch or crease. With the single-minded determination typical of a resolved adolescent, she convinced her mother that it was prudent to move all of her fragile ballet belongings into the new house before anything else.

That the house wasn't actually new, but an old farmhouse that had been renovated after much of it had been destroyed by fire a few years back, didn't bother Sherri, her mother or her stepfather. Soon the whole family was absorbed in the taxing process of the move.

Yet on the opening day of moving, when mother and daughter staggered into Sherri's room under handfuls of ballerina posters, the family received the first hint that there was something in the house not included in the rental agreement. Sherri recalls today: "There wasn't anything in the house; we hadn't moved one box in yet.

My mother and I went up to my room to hang posters up. I walked across the floor and turned around to ask her how a particular poster would look up on that wall. It was then that we both noticed this 5"-by-7" black and white photograph lying there in the middle of the room—we both would have sworn that the room was empty before I crossed the floor. It was a black and white of a man we'd never seen before; it looked like an author's headshot for a cover of a book. On the back of the picture, on the upper left-hand corner, 'Mr. Enoch' was written in very neat handwriting. It was not the name of the owners we had rented from. We didn't know who it was. And we both knew that the picture wasn't there just seconds ago when I first walked into the room."

Something about the picture perturbed Sherri's mom, but she shrugged off whatever uneasiness she felt and tossed the photograph on the floor. They were just about to leave after hanging up all the posters when, almost as an afterthought, Sherri's mother picked up the picture and took it downstairs, where she laid it on the kitchen counter. Even in the ensuing days, as boxes began piling into the new home and all the family's possessions were in complete disarray, Sherri's mom was always conscious of the picture of Mr. Enoch on the kitchen counter. "My mom finally just took the picture and shoved it behind a box, just to get it out of her sight," Sherri recalls today. "Well, it showed up on top of that same box the next day."

After that, Sherri's mother, by now thoroughly spooked, tossed Mr. Enoch into the garbage. When the photograph reappeared on the kitchen counter later on that day, Sherri's mother—perhaps in an attempt to preserve her mental well-being—tried to assume that her husband or daughter had dug it out of the garbage and put it back on the counter. She told her husband that the picture didn't belong to them, but was left behind by someone who had lived in the house before, and threw it away again, this time making sure to bury it deep in the trash can. It reappeared on the kitchen counter again the following day, and Sherri's mom decided she had enough. She burned the picture.

Though the photograph of Mr. Enoch was never seen again, it was quickly becoming evident to the whole family that there were a number of other bizarre things going on in the house. "Doors you knew you had left open were shut when you returned, and vice-versa, doors that you had closed would open by themselves. At night, my mother would hear music coming from music boxes when we didn't have any music boxes in the house. If you left empty glasses in the living room, there would be warm clear water in them when you walked back in."

But somehow Sherri wasn't too disturbed with what was happening. "I always felt like I was being watched, especially when I was upstairs." Sherri admits that the presence sometimes made her feel nervous, but for the most part, she was actually quite comfortable with the unseen sentinel that resided in the house.

As for Sherri's mother, after she got over the initial shock of Mr. Enoch's photograph, not only was she able to cope with the ghost in the house, but she actually felt good that it was around. Whenever she got that sense of someone being in the room, a warm, comfortable feeling came over her. "My mother would hear footsteps coming up the stairs at night," Sherri recalls. "The steps would never go back down the stairs or never even walk down the hall; it was like whoever it was just stood there at the top of the stairs." Perhaps the feeling Sherri's mother got from the watchful presence in the hall might be best described as a sense of security—a feeling that something or someone that cared was watching over her.

The same could not be said for her husband, however. Sherri remembers the contrast in her mother's and her stepfather's attitude towards the place. "My stepfather never felt comfortable in the house. He won't describe it any way other than that—other than to say that it was not like being 'watched'—but more like he was in danger."

Often when Sherri's mother and stepfather would sit together in the living room, her stepfather would complain about how cold the room was while her mother would be reclining in the couch warm and comfortable. At the request of her grumbling husband, Sherri's mother would switch places with her spouse, only to have the same climatic deviations in the room continue. He would spend as little time as he could in the house by himself. If there was nobody else at home, he would make up any excuse to be outside, finding something to tinker with in the garage, or embarking on long walks on the property until somebody came home. Whatever sympathy Sherri and her mother had for the man of the house, it wasn't until the ghost came between mother and daughter that the family decided to leave.

The relationship between Sherri and her mother was in transition. Sherri was at an age when she began to resent the parental rituals that seemed to confine her to childhood, whereas her mother, conscious of her daughter's approaching adulthood, was having difficulty letting go of the child she once knew. "I would hear her enter the room and feel her cover me at night," Sherri recalls. "Or on some nights, she would just stand at the door and watch me for a while before going back to bed."

Sherri loved her mother dearly, but was somewhat resentful at what she saw as her mother's over-bearing conduct. She finally confronted her about the nightly visits one morning at the breakfast table. "I'm 16 years old, mother. You do not have to come to my room to check on me every night. And if I'm uncovered, it means that I'm hot—so please don't cover me back up."

She was shocked to find half the family's belongings packed away in cardboard boxes when she got home from school that day. "Pack up your posters, honey," Sherri's mother told her, "we're moving." They were completely packed up and gone in a week, having lived in the house for less than a year. Only after they had settled into their new place did Sherri's mother tell her that she had never once checked on her at night while they lived in the house.

Sherri's family had taken the house on a one-year lease while they were waiting for their own home to be built. Because they moved before their lease was up, they sublet the house to tenants who would rent for the remainder of the lease, with the condition that Sherri's family could keep their large refrigerator in the garage so they wouldn't have to move it twice. Sherri describes an encounter her stepfather had with one of these new tenants when he eventually went back for the fridge. "The people came out and asked my stepdad, 'Did anything odd happen when you lived here?' My stepfather, afraid that if he confirmed their suspicions they might break the lease and leave us with two rent payments, told them no."

Sherri's stepfather definitely knew better, and though curiosity impelled him to ask what "odd things" they were referring to exactly, the tenants left it at that and helped him move the fridge. Soon after, Sherri's family moved into their new home, custom built for them and thus devoid of other people's ghosts. Who knows what other experiences future tenants had in Mr. Enoch's household? Besides Sherri, no one else has spoken up about the renovated farmhouse outside of Battle Creek.

Guardian Angel?

In many respects, the differences between religious experience and supernatural phenomenon might boil down to a matter of perspective. For instance, some might see little difference between a benevolent ghost on one hand and a guardian angel on the other. Indeed, the idea of concerned spirits giving comfort to distressed mortals is so prevalent in human folklore that it has spanned a good number of religions and cultures. So it is that here, the term "guardian angel" is used to identify spirits that have been known as Valkyries, Boddhisatvas and Avatars in different times and places. But for Janet Delitka, a faithful Roman Catholic who resides in Leonard, Michigan, the generous presence that eased her mind, comforted her family and saved her very life during the hard trials of 1998 is a divine messenger from a Christian God—her guardian angel.

In her letter to the June 2001 issue of *FATE* magazine, Delitka explains that her troubles began early in the summer of 1998, when her husband informed her that "the confines of marriage were too much for him" and he wanted a divorce. It wasn't an amicable separation, and as the harsh battles of marital separation proceeded, Janet Delitka's mental and emotional health began to deteriorate. By August, the continuous strain of battling with her husband, taking care of her children and adjusting to her new life as a single mom finally took a physical toll on her. Janet became sick.

It was on an August night, after she had fallen into a fitful sleep, that Janet first sensed the other presence. She woke in the middle of the evening to find a woman standing by her, crying into her hands hysterically. Janet quickly sat up in her bed, at which point the woman began speaking, spilling out frantic words through barely restrained sobs. To this day, Delitka cannot remember what the figure was saying, only that her message was very serious. Neither does Janet remember how the encounter was concluded, but when she woke the next morning she was pressed with an overriding need to see a doctor as soon as possible.

She was in her doctor's office that day, demanding that she be given a Pap test. The physician tried to speak to her reasonably, insisting that whatever she was currently suffering from was a result of the stress from her divorce. He also reminded her that she had just recently had the procedure done, so this time it wouldn't be covered by her medical insurance. Nothing the man said made a difference to Janet, and she made him go ahead with the procedure. He called her two days later, telling her the test results were abnormal, and she needed to have a biopsy.

One week later, Janet's doctor was trying to figure out how to break the devastating news to his distraught patient that she had tested positive for an extremely virulent strain of cervical cancer and her life was in imminent danger. But there still was hope for her. The doctor was amazed at Delitka's intuition about what was happening to her body. "How did you know?" he asked Janet just after he gave her the brutal diagnosis.

She was too stunned to reply and only looked uncomprehendingly at her physician. "Right now, we have a fighting chance against the cancer," the doctor began. "If you had not insisted on that Pap smear, I can tell you right now that you wouldn't be alive to see your next birthday."

Janet was still silent.

"Do you believe in God?" the doctor asked.

The question snapped her out of her frightened confusion. "Yes, I do believe in God."

"Good," he responded, "because He believes in you."

These last encouraging words bounced off Janet as she made her way out of the doctor's office. The thought of the next 14 days cast a long shadow over her at that moment, and she wasn't sure if she could see anything past the looming fear of the coming two weeks. In that time she had to move with her children, finalize the divorce with her soon-to-be-ex husband, and undergo a major operation for her cancer.

She almost didn't make it through the first week. The accumulating pressures took their toll when Janet found herself in her new home, standing in a living room full of boxes, reassuring her six-year-old son that she wasn't going to die. After hugging the boy and tucking him into bed, she went up to her bedroom and collapsed on the floor—supplicating to God through desperate tears for some kind of reprieve from her crippling anxiety. She didn't feel that she had the strength to go on. There was the adjustment to the sudden dissolution to her family life, the turmoil of moving herself and her two children to a new home, and the legal battles for child support. All this would have been enough for anyone to take on, but the thought of her upcoming battle with cancer on top of everything else was the proverbial last straw.

It was then, at her darkest moment, as Janet desperately prayed for divine intervention, that a hand fell on her shoulder. Sudden warmth spread from that shoulder through her entire body. In another second she was completely calm; all the emotions that had been tormenting her over the last few days dissolved into nothingness, and all that she knew at that moment was an overwhelming sense of peace. She turned around to see who was standing beside her, but saw only empty space: there was nobody there. Instantly exhausted, Janet Delitka crawled into her bed and fell asleep.

The same apparition who had visited her about a week earlier came back that night. This time she was sitting on the bed, smiling at Janet, gently stroking her hair and speaking quietly. She told her that there was nothing to be afraid of—that everything was going to be all right.

Janet cannot remember when the woman left, but when she woke up the next morning, it was as if the dark clouds brewing over her for the past months had suddenly dissolved into bright blue sky. She was filled with newfound energy. After breakfast, Janet played hide-and-seek with her children among the boxes and unassembled furniture of their new house. The cheer that had been absent from Janet and her children's lives for so many days returned with the sounds of giggling and laughing that filled their new home. Family members arriving shortly after to help unpack instantly noticed the new mood in Delitka's household. At first, they did not know what to make of this cheer, as they themselves were having a hard time coping with all the difficulties that had fallen so suddenly on Janet's head. But her uplifting attitude was contagious, and before long everyone around her was buoyed with a new sense of hope.

Having been fortunate enough to undergo her operation when the cancer was still in its early stages, Janet came out of the surgery just fine. Her oncologist was impressed with how soon her cancer was detected and removed. He pointed out how lucky she was to have become aware of the cancer so early, as it was virtually symptom-less in its early stages and almost always fatal in its final stages. But Janet wasn't so sure that her recovery was completely dependent on "luck." She told her doctor about the kindly woman in her dreams and how those dreams may have saved her life. Her physician looked at her thoughtfully before saying, "Are you sure they were dreams?" As of yet, Janet Delitka has not been able to give her doctor a certain answer, but her faith in God and His host of angels has never been more solid than it is today.

The Lady in Black

The summer of 1995 was a time of shattered dreams and hard transition for Larry. He and his wife had just ended their long marriage in an ugly, drawn-out divorce; his children—cubs no longer—finally earned the means for independence and left his broken home to start their own lives; and the company he worked for was considering relocating him from his home in Belleville to a distant town in sparsely populated northern Michigan. All Larry could do was watch as the mantle of security he had been working to build throughout most of his life was blown away by the cruel winds of circumstance. While an optimist may have looked at these events as an opportunity for a new lease on life, the 40-some years Larry had been on this earth dissuaded him from any such hope, and he found himself plummeting into a deep, dark depression.

Who knows how far Larry would have fallen if it were not for the company of Stacy Kendricks? Meeting Stacy a few months after his divorce was finalized, he found a sympathetic ear and compassionate heart in the single mother of two. Stacy was reeling from a difficult divorce of her own, and there is no doubt that the couple's attraction to each other sprang largely from the shared rubble of their pasts. Mutual support turned to love, and before long they were engaged to be married.

But it would not be a cheery courtship. Most of Larry's visits to Ms. Kendrick's Belleville home were lengthy lamentations on the direction of his life. Memories of his ex-wife were still fresh, his move north was imminent, and there were no family or friends there whom he could rely upon for comfort. Stacy would be as supportive of Larry as she could, yet he was often inconsolable, leaving his fiancée racked with worry by the time he would leave. It was then, after Larry would depart, that the despair he left behind seemed to take on a life of its own.

As Stacy lay in bed, wondering what she could do to ease her beau's troubles, her thoughts would be interrupted by strange, unexplainable noises. Reverend Gerald S. Hunter interviewed Stacy in his book *Haunted Michigan*.

"Almost every time after he would leave, I would begin to hear movement down in my basement...it sounded like someone was down there moving things around—I could hear boxes being shoved around, and heavy footsteps slapping against the concrete floor."

It was an unfinished basement, only used for laundry and storage...and there was no way that the family's housecat, which slept downstairs at night, was able to make those kind of noises. Yet for reasons she could not explain, Stacy was not frightened in the least.

"Sometimes I'd get up and go open the basement door. Invariably the noise would stop, and my cat...would fly up the stairs in a panic and go hide somewhere until morning. It reached a point where I couldn't even get him to go back down there, and he got so nervous that he began to lose his fur."

But at that time, there was too much going on in Stacy's life to give the mysterious noises coming from her basement much more than passing thought. The daylight hours were hectic, laden with the duties of looking after her two daughters and working full time. Meanwhile, Larry was getting worse, and his evening visits were leaving her more emotionally distraught than ever. It was at that point when the enigmatic presence in the basement moved upstairs.

Tired, worried and sleepless, Stacy was tossing and turning in bed one night when she saw a large shadowy figure of a man walk past her doorway in the hall outside her bedroom. He was visible for only a second from where she was lying, and Stacy blinked in disbelief, wondering if her eyes were playing tricks on her. They were not.

Her stare remained locked on the doorway in silent anticipation, and before long, the looming silhouette had come back to her door. This time it was standing at the doorway, looking in…and in the utter silence of the next moment, walked into her room, passed the foot of her bed and stopped between her and the window, staring down at where she lay. Most people would freak out, yet just as with the disturbances in her basement, Stacy was not scared at all. In fact, she actually felt comforted by the towering presence. A long-forgotten sense of calm washed over her as she silently stared up at the figure. He stood there for several minutes before turning to leave—not saying a word. A few minutes later, she had fallen into a deep, peaceful sleep.

The visits continued over the next few weeks, growing evermore personal. A few times, the moonlight through her bedroom window gave Stacy a good look at her nightly visitor. And she found herself surprised at the humanness of his features. Stacy described him as "a good looking man of about 60 with a receding hairline and a beautiful smile." Sometimes she would wake from a fitful sleep to see the figure sitting at the edge of her bed and holding her hand. Unlike most accounts of physical contact with the supernatural, Stacy reports that his touch was not icy, but warm…and she was able to make out his features.

She was not afraid of him at all, feeling instead that he was there to give her comfort, letting her know that she didn't have to worry about Larry. He felt like family.

It was not long before it dawned on her that the figure was Larry's father, who had died a few years back. True, she had never met the man, nor had she ever seen any pictures of him, but the feeling was too strong to ignore. Her hunch was confirmed when Larry showed her a photograph of his dad, and she joyfully informed her fiancé of the calming support the spirit of his father had been lending. It was a desperate time for Larry, and he recalls that he did not have the strength for skepticism, grateful as he was for any help.

Yet Larry's father would not be the only ghost to haunt Stacy's home on Fairbanks Street. If Larry's distress attracted a benevolent apparition in his time of need, it seems his weakness had baited another, less munificent phantom as well.

Stacy was watching the rear lights of Larry's car disappear after an evening's visit and was just closing the drapes when she first saw her. A woman was standing at the corner of her driveway, staring at Stacy's house. She was dressed completely in black and a long hooded cape was drawn around her head, obscuring her visage. Something about the woman struck terror into Ms. Kendricks's heart. Paralyzed with fear, Stacy stared in horror as the woman lingered for several moments, then turned and continued down the sidewalk. The woman began appearing on the driveway regularly, eerily staring at Stacy's home after Larry's late visits.

For a time, Larry had been spared any run-ins with the

weird denizen on Fairbanks Street, but on a hot, muggy night later that summer, he would have the most unsettling experience of all. He relates his eerie encounter in Reverend Hunter's book:

"Well, one night I came over for a visit and I was really depressed. My move was coming soon, I missed my kids, and I was really ready to give up. Stacy and I talked for a couple of hours, and I remember blaming God for all my problems and getting really angry. About that time, I remembered I'd left a gift I had bought for Stacy out in my car, so I went out to get it."

It was some time after midnight when Larry went to get Stacy's present. The rain that had been falling for the last few hours had just let up, and the air was hot and humid. Larry had just stepped out of his car when he first caught a glimpse of her. "As I'm walking down the center of Fairbanks back toward Stacy's, I notice movement out of the corner of my eye. I looked over at the sidewalk to my left, and there was this woman, a large woman, walking down the sidewalk parallel to me, heading in the same direction. Right away, I knew something wasn't right, because an instant earlier there was no one to be seen, but here was this woman practically right next to me. For some reason, I got the strong feeling that she only had the appearance of being human, because I could plainly hear my footsteps slapping against the wet pavement, but her footsteps were perfectly silent."

Stacy had told him about the woman in black, and Larry was overcome with curiosity, quickening his pace so he would intercept the woman before she arrived in front of Stacy's. He ended up cutting her off right at the

The lady in black appeared several times as an evil presence.

corner of the driveway. "When I stopped, she also stopped, and stared back at me. She was dressed in a long, black cape that tied at her neck and spilled down to her ankles. The cape was hooded, so I couldn't see her hair, but I got a good look at her face."

If there was nothing so spectacular or otherworldly about the woman's appearance, the leaden feeling in the pit of his stomach suggested she was much more than she appeared. "She was very plain looking," Larry continued, "with a round face and very dark, round eyes. She wore no makeup, and the look on her face was calm and serene. She simply stood there and stared at me, showing no emotion at all. Her arms were folded, and her hands were tucked inside her cape."

Though no words passed between the two, Larry knew that she was waiting for him to speak, that she herself could not start the conversation. But Larry found himself frozen before her, silenced by an instinctual urge to simply get away from this woman as quickly as he could. "I…knew that if I spoke I would somehow be giving myself to this woman, and I'd never be the same again. The feeling that I got was that she was evil personified."

Without wasting another moment, he turned and headed for Stacy's door, going as fast as he could without breaking into a run.

As soon as he was inside, Larry ran to Stacy's front window to see if the woman was still there, just catching a glimpse of her as she continued down the sidewalk. Seized by a sudden, completely irrational impulse, Larry decided to chase her down, much to the dismay of his frightened fiancée. Yet by the time he got back out onto the sidewalk, she was nowhere to be seen.

Soon after, Larry made his move upstate; and with Stacy's long-distance support, adjusted quite well to his new conditions. Things began getting better for him. As for Stacy, she received no more nocturnal visitations— either from Larry's father or from the pale apparition on her driveway. She came to believe that these ghosts were awakened by her fiancé's desperation, that the lady in black was there to somehow claim Larry during his time of spiritual vulnerability.

But it turned out that Larry's move north was just what he needed. With new work in a new environment, the pain of his past lost its edge, and he began building a new life in earnest. Stacy sold her house in Belleville and moved her family north to join her new husband. There have been no further reports of the ghost of Larry's father, or the woman in black on Fairbanks Street.

Not Happy With the Renovations

Those of us who have spent any time sweating through home renovations know quite well the distinct kind of pain they can be. Hammering, puttying, painting, stripping, sanding, waxing, gluing, tearing down…the vocabulary of renovation evokes images of roomfuls of cardboard boxes, projects that almost always drag on longer than expected and results that seem to come far too slowly for the amount of elbow grease expended. So imagine what it would be like, if in addition to the obstacles that are inherent in remodeling, you were working in a place housing a ghost that was doing everything that it could to confound your efforts.

Such was the case for a family living on South River Road in a farmhouse just south of the small town of Gladwin in central Michigan. While researching material for his book *Haunted Michigan,* Reverend Gerald S. Hunter encountered Fran and Allen Boucher (pseudonyms) in August 1997. Recalling the huge remodeling operation they went through in the summer of 1989, the Bouchers still get a haunted look in their eyes.

The couple was happy enough with the size of the old Depression-era farmhouse they had purchased a few years back, as it gave their energetic children more than enough room to run around in. But the interior was a little shabby, and the two took on a serious renovating project.

They weren't far into remodeling the upstairs bedrooms when things started to get strange. Actually, the first indication of a paranormal presence was almost welcomed by

Fran and Allen, The couple was busy tearing out old carpet and putting up 4'-by-8' drywall in the sweltering summer heat. Sweating buckets and cursing the mugginess of the Michigan summer, the Bouchers must have believed that they were hallucinating the first time the temperature in the bedrooms plummeted. It was a welcome relief indeed, but when it got so cold that condensation trails formed around their mouths and nostrils, the couple wasn't sure what to think.

Yet with the second floor of their home in absolute disarray, Fran and Allen were not willing to waste much thought on anything that didn't have to do with their remodeling. Bundling up under extra layers, they pressed ahead in the bedrooms for the next few weeks. More clothing, however, would not help them deal with the bizarre events to come.

Not long after the inexplicable temperature changes, things began to disappear. And not just any "things," but tools that were crucial for the renovations to continue. "We took forever to hang the drywall in those rooms," Fran told Hunter. "We'd go up there to work, and sometimes the drywall screws would be gone, and then the next day maybe it would be the drywall tape or the drywall mud. It seemed like something or somebody just didn't want the walls covered with drywall."

Allen was having similar problems with his own tools. "I'd get home from work, eat supper and then head upstairs for the evening." Things would start just fine, but before long it was evident that the invisible thief was interested in more than just drywall material. "I'd reach for one of my tools—one I had just been using—and it would be gone.

I began to lose screwdrivers, hammers and even my staple gun. And I had been the only one up there at the time."

Allen was annoyed with having to constantly lumber down to the basement to look for replacement tools, and his frustration continued to mount until he made a startling discovery. He was in the basement, cursing under his breath and rummaging through his toolbox for a screwdriver he had just lost when a glint of light coming from atop a ceiling support beam caught his eye. Stepping up on a chair to take a look at what was there, he found every tool he had lost since the renovations began arranged neatly side by side on top of the beam. From then on, whenever one of his tools went missing, he would immediately make his way down to the basement where, without fail, that same tool would be sitting on top of the ceiling support beam. Allen definitely found the whole affair quite disconcerting, but the man made a fine show of human adaptability, and quickly got used to the daily jaunts down to the basement for tools he was holding in his hands a few seconds previous.

The next supernatural manifestation in the house was a little harder to adjust to. It first appeared when Fran began gutting the storage room that she intended to make into a sewing room. She was by herself in the house, moving boxes out of the room and stacking them in the hallway when her work was interrupted by a man who suddenly appeared in the doorway. He looked to be about 40 years old, was thin, and wore faded coveralls, a plaid shirt and had winter boots on, although the temperature outside was well above 80 degrees. He seemed to be staring right through her. "I knew instantly that he wasn't real," Fran told Reverend Hunter, "that he wasn't alive." The man stood there for a few moments, then gave her a disgusted look and turned and walked away. Apparently, he didn't like what they were doing with the house.

Fran was so spooked by the incident that she ran downstairs and called her mother. By the time she heard her mother's voice on the telephone, she calmed down somewhat, and decided not to tell her about the man in the doorway. Fran didn't want her mother to think she had lost her mind, after all—but hearing her mother's voice did much to alleviate her immediate fear. It wouldn't be the last time that this man appeared before the Bouchers.

Allen and Trisha, one of his daughters, were in the basement bringing up some clean laundry when the man appeared again. The two were turning away from the dryer with an armload of laundry each when they saw him standing in the partial darkness of the room. "He was staring at us, with a look on his face like he didn't approve of us being down there," Allen remembered. "I watched him for a moment, looked over at Trisha to see if she saw him too—which she did—and then looked back. He was still there, watching us. Without saying a word, we both headed for the stairs." Both of them looked back into the basement when they were at the top of the stairs. The man still stood there, silently staring up at them with a malevolent look on his face. Allen flicked off the basement light and shut the door.

From that day on, the dark unfinished basement became the eerie abode of the renovation ghost that was haunting the Boucher home. He would always stand in the same place, looming in the shadows by the coal bin door staring silently at whoever had the misfortune of venturing down there at that moment. It was not long before the family started avoiding the basement completely, and dirty laundry began to build up in the household.

Fran and Allen tried to keep the haunting a secret, telling their children that good people didn't speak of such things, but apparently the man in the basement had plans of his own. One day they had family over for a birthday party for one of the girls. Allen recalls, "It was after dinner and all the kids were out playing while the adults were sitting in the living room drinking coffee and eating ice cream." Fran and Allen were doing their best to talk about anything but the renovations when the heavy sound of big footsteps coming down the stairs ended all conversation in the room.

All the people in the room turned their heads to the doorway that opened up onto the staircase, wondering who the unknown guest was. Meanwhile Fran and Allen's thoughts on what was about to transpire were closer to horror than curiosity—they knew exactly what was coming down the stairs.

And in the next moment he appeared: the stern-looking man in the overalls was standing in the doorway, surveying the suddenly silent room with gimlet-eyed resentment. Somebody dropped a teaspoon. He took a few steps into the room, then turned back around and walked out the way he came and into the Bouchers' bedroom. Allen, outraged that this specter had the gall to appear when they were entertaining guests, bolted out of his chair and into the bedroom, hoping that he could confront the spirit once and for all. He was joined by a cousin who apparently believed the ghost was a mortal intruder. Of course by the time the two men had run into the room, there was nobody there.

Struggling for explanations, the Bouchers could no longer hide the fact that their house was haunted. While some family members at the birthday party took the news in stride, others flatly stated that they wouldn't come back to the house unless something was done about the apparition. It turns out that all they had to do to get rid of the ghost was finish the renovations.

Try as he might to stop the remodeling, the ghost was ultimately unsuccessful in halting the Bouchers' plans. And when the work on the house was finally finished, the phantom disappeared. Now everyone enjoys the crisp new look of the home...but the Bouchers are definitely going to think twice before embarking on any more renovations.

Chapter 5

Specters on the Lakes

★ ★ ★

Much of Michigan's supernatural folklore is tied to the Great Lakes. Certainly stories of frontier battles, homicides, suicides and all other sorts of human misery abound in the state's interior, but most of Michigan's legends are waterlogged dramas on the stormy waters of Lake Superior, Lake Huron, Lake Erie and Lake Michigan. These cruel reservoirs have sent innumerable ships to the bottom, stealing fortunes, breaking hearts and ending lives. Laden with mortal tragedy, the deathly lakes have become haunted by the indelible presence of restless spirits who seem to believe that their relegation to Davy Jones's Locker came before their allotted years had passed.

Among the numerous tales of ghost ships, phantom fur traders and spectral sailors, perhaps the most frequent reports of hauntings come from the many lighthouses that dot Michigan's coastline. Maybe these towers, shining in the night, were the last things that many men and women saw before they drowned, and so became the focus of bitter spirits resentful of their watery graves. And then there are the reports of lighthouse keepers who continue to linger over their stations long after their earthly days have expired. These were men either driven mad by the loneliness of their work, left heartbroken by personal tragedy, or so fixated by the routine of their daily duties that they could not let them go even after they were dead and buried.

Big Bay Point

The lighthouse at Big Bay Point on Michigan's Northern Peninsula seems to be a particularly strong magnet for wayward souls of the undead. Though the light station was built in 1896, reports of strange occurrences have begun only just recently. Ever since one cold fall night in 1986, when Norman Gotschall was awakened by a violent banging just outside the house, supernatural activity seems to have come to life in the building. Once-restful spirits have flocked to the lonely light station, sending cold chills of fright through the building's residents on more than one occasion. While we can only guess at why haunted activity stepped up after 1991, the history of the lighthouse is certainly dark enough to merit the presence of lost souls.

William Prior, the lighthouse's first keeper, had no way of knowing that the values he lived by would usher heartrending tragedy into his life. A hard, uncompromising man, Prior went about his duties on the lighthouse as if work was the only thing that mattered. Not only did he push himself hard, but he expected the same of those around him and was a ruthlessly demanding employer.

In April 1901, Prior's son accidentally cut himself while working on the station's dock. It was a bad wound, but Will Prior, busy under his full schedule, delayed getting his son the medical attention he needed. Three months had passed by the time young Prior was taken to the hospital in Marquette, but by then, it was too late. The cut was heavily infected, and gangrene had begun to do its work. A few days later, Will's son was dead.

Big Bay Point Lighthouse and nearby shoreline

Racked with guilt and grief, Will became a babbling mess after the funeral. He did not last a single day when he got back to his work at the lighthouse. Early in the morning on the day following his return, the lighthouse keeper disappeared into the woods with a gun and some strychnine. No one believed that he was going off for a hunt.

Three months later, on September 24, searchers found what was left of William Prior. He was hanging from a maple tree, his decaying remains dangling by a grotesquely lengthened neck amidst a swarm of flies. Even then, a look of guilt-ridden sorrow was evident on his face.

A new keeper was hired soon after, and the lighthouse at Big Bay Point was manned without incident until 1941, when the Coast Guard automated the station. The lighthouse was abandoned for 20 years, and then passed through a succession of owners until it finally ended up in the hands of a group headed by a man named Norman

Gotschall in 1985. Gotschall's crew began renovations, making the lighthouse into a bed and breakfast. During Gotschall's initial night in the building the first of a series of eerie incidents occurred.

Gotschall was nestled in his bed as an icy northwest wind buffeted the walls outside and moaned through the empty rooms of the Big Bay light. He was just beginning to drift off when a violent clamor outside sent him bolting out of bed and scurrying for his clothes. It sounded as if something large had crashed against the building or the wind had torn doors or shutters off their hinges; the banging got louder as he made his way to the main entrance. But the instant he flung the door open and stepped outside to survey the damage, he was greeted by absolute calm. Not only was there no evidence of any harm to the lighthouse, but even the air was still—without the slightest trace of a breeze. Profoundly shaken by the sudden quiet, Gotschall tossed and turned for the rest of the night, more disturbed by this unnatural silence than he was by the earlier gale.

A few days later, a cleaning woman Gotschall had hired came running up the stairs from the basement, terror in her eyes. "Who's in the shower down there?" was all she was able to say to her employer. Gotschall went downstairs to investigate, but the shower was neither on nor occupied. He let the matter drop, wondering what had gotten the woman so riled up, and if it had anything to do with the goings on a few nights back.

A rattled couple at the bed and breakfast had told Gotschall about a bearded man dressed in an old Lighthouse Service uniform walking the grounds. They assumed that he was one of the hotel staff and called the man over, but as the

Big Bay Point Lighthouse in winter

image of the keeper got closer, they noticed that he was slightly transparent. Approaching deliberately, the apparition had a blank look on its face, as if it was looking straight through them. He kept walking until he got within a few feet of the petrified couple and then vanished right before them.

It was then that it clicked for Gotschall. Familiar with the history of the lighthouse, he suspected that the ghostly figure and the inexplicable events were related to the tragic deaths of William Prior and his son. But he could not understand why there were no previous accounts of Prior's ghost. While the private owners of the building over the past few decades might have had sufficient reason to keep the hauntings quiet, the lighthouse had been manned for a full 40 years by various keepers who had not said a word about any ghostly activity.

His suspicions about Prior's ghost were confirmed when a psychic he hired to investigate the building claimed that a man with a beard and hat materialized at the foot of her bed. Her description of the apparition sounded almost identical to the tortured old keeper. The woman also told Gotschall that she spoke with the man's spirit; Prior was dismayed at the condition of the lighthouse, and would be unable to rest until the light was restored to proper working order. Gotschall lobbied the Coast Guard to return a light beacon to the tower and was eventually awarded with a fully functional light in 1990. But the hauntings did not end.

Gotschall and his partners sold the lighthouse to John Gale and Linda and Jeff Gamble in 1991, the same trio who run the bed and breakfast today. If Gotschall thought he had solved the problem with the new beacon, it became obvious over time that the restored light had only attracted more spirits. Supernatural activity increased under the new management, and a visiting paranormal expert informed Gale and the Gambles that there was not one, but five ghosts drifting through the lighthouse's halls. The ghost hunter claimed that four of the spirits were friendly, but one was considerably angry. While the owners were quite certain that old Will Prior was one of the spirits, they had no clue about the other four.

The first incident took place in the spring of 1994. It happened one night when three couples were spending the night at the inn: a husband and wife and the wife's mother were staying upstairs, while two couples were downstairs on the main floor. One of the couples from the main floor went to bed early, while the other two went into town for dinner. The couple upstairs went for a walk at about 10 PM, while the woman's mother stayed in with a book. Linda Gamble, aware that two couples were still out, went to sleep without locking the doors.

She was awakened by the telephone ringing at 2 AM. It was the young couple from downstairs; they were locked out. Assuming that the couple that went for a walk had locked the doors when they came back, Linda got up to let her two guests in, thinking it strange that the pair upstairs would lock all the doors into the building. But the next morning at breakfast, the couple staying upstairs asked Mrs. Gamble why she had locked them out. They explained that after they got back from their walk, they had to call up to the woman's mother to come down and let them in. And they claimed they did not lock the door behind them, knowing that the young couple was still out. The other couple downstairs had not left their room through the entire night.

Linda resorted to the supernatural to explain the situation. Frederick Stonehouse quotes her in *Haunted Lakes*: "The couples really convinced me that they had no idea about the locked doors. All I know is that the room the loud couple was in was the old keeper's office. They were in there laughing and drinking before they went out; maybe he didn't like it and decided to lock them out."

When Linda discovered that all the windows had been locked that night as well, she became convinced that something weird was going on.

The second incident happened later that year. A couple had checked in at about 9:30 PM. Exhausted from their long day of driving, the man went directly to bed, while the woman thought she would go through the lighthouse's library before she slept. She ended up reading late into the evening, and it was well past midnight by the time she began making her way back to her suite. Lighting the way with a flashlight she had brought with her, the woman gently opened the door to her room, careful not to wake her husband, and quietly walked into the bathroom, placing the flashlight on the sink. Stepping up to look into the mirror, she almost screamed at what she saw in the reflection. A man with a full, grizzled beard and wearing a hat was standing behind her, staring blankly. When she spun around to confront the intruder, there was no one there.

A newlywed couple also had a strange encounter in that same room. They were taking a shower when the radio they had on suddenly cut out. There was nothing wrong with the power, and everything else was still running; the radio alone just stopped playing. Shortly after, the couple settled into bed. The woman asked her husband to turn off the light, and just as he was reaching over to switch off the lamp, the light went out on its own.

Incidents such as these have continued at the lighthouse. Doors open and close, lights switch on and off, and William Prior has been spotted on the grounds, at the foot of people's beds and at the head of the stairs—always at night. The keepers of the inn have called in psychics on occasion, who have confirmed the earlier belief that five spirits were dwelling on Big Bay Point. One of the investigators claimed that the angry spirit of a young woman lives on the second floor of the light—she is chagrined because nobody knows she is there. Apparently, the psychic had a conversation with this spirit and learned that the woman died in the lighthouse during the late 1950s when the place was abandoned. Nothing more was learned about the details of her death. Why she has only recently begun to haunt the lighthouse is not known.

The other three spirits are still something of a mystery. In his book *Haunted Lakes*, Stonehouse speculates that they could be wandering souls of the crew that died on the steamship *Iosco* and the schooner-barge *Olive Jeanette* during a vicious squall in September 1905. Both ships went down with all hands near the Huron Islands just west of Big Bay Point. Perhaps the souls of these men came flocking to the lighthouse after Gotschall put the light back into the tower at Big Bay, drawn to the last thing they saw during the final moments of their lives.

Point aux Barques

The sun had not yet risen on the morning of April 23, 1880, when the captain of the scow *J.H. Magruder* ordered a red light to be hung in the rigging of his ship. The *Magruder* was in distress, taking in water just off the Point aux Barques reef on the tip of Michigan's thumb. The captain feared the worst as the frigid Lake Huron water slowly filled his badly listing boat. Not only did he stand to lose his cargo of 187,000 feet of lumber, but the lives of his crew, his wife and his two children were in very real jeopardy. Turning his back on the people whose well-being rested in his hands, the captain looked towards the Point aux Barques Lighthouse. The veneer of easy confidence he kept up for the sake of his wards melted into obvious anxiety as his eyes fell on the singular beam of light rotating at the top of the solitary tower. He then looked up to the small red beacon that hung from his own boat, and if anyone was standing close enough at that moment, they would have heard a silent prayer come from the old salt's grizzled lips.

James Nantau was the watchman on duty at the Point aux Barques station that night, and he reported the red light to his superior, Jerome Kiah, almost the moment that he saw it. By the time Kiah rushed up to the lookout point, a heavy gray dawn was rising over the lake. Looking through his telescope, he saw the crippled *Magruder* anchored just outside the reef, a distress flag flying at half-mast next to the red lantern. "All hands were immediately called," Kiah would testify in the investigation that followed, "and we promptly ran the boat out onto the dock."

The crew of seven on the lifeboat were all experienced seamen, and they rowed their way across the shore surf and over the reef, barely breaking a sweat. It was after they cleared the reef that things took a turn for the worse.

"We found the water on the other side of the reef heavier than we had expected," Kiah would later say, "but still not so heavy as we had experienced on other occasions." Alas, Lake Huron is famous for its bad temper and in the next moment Jerome Kiah was struggling to stay afloat as the suddenly angered waters roared over the gunwales of the lifeboat. "I saw a tremendous breaker coming for us and I barely had time to head for it, when it broke over our stern and filled us." Kiah immediately gave the order to start bailing the water out, but the crewmen were hardly able to start before another wave crashed over them. With instincts born from years of experience with the waters of the Great Lakes, the crewmen braced themselves for what they knew was about to come: the next wave hit them hard, capsizing their boat and throwing everyone aboard into Huron's icy cold drink.

The capable crew did not panic but immediately set about righting the overturned vessel. No sooner were they back in and afloat when another breaker capsized them again. Once more, the beleaguered seamen righted the boat, only to be overturned by the unforgiving waters for a third time. Kiah stated that this sequence of capsize and recovery repeated itself several times before the men finally found themselves frozen, soaked and sapped of any strength to roll the boat again. Clinging to the lifelines on the side of the boat, the exhausted sailors could do nothing more than hold on for dear life as the freezing waters buffeted them and their turtled vessel. One by one, hypothermia claimed the men huddled against the lethal fury of Lake Huron; Kiah tried shouting encouragement to his fading crew, reminding them of friends and family that waited for them on dry land, but the situation was beyond remedy. Numb fingers loosened their grip on ropes and, each in their turn, the men drifted away into oblivion. By the time the boat washed ashore some two to three hours later, Kiah was the only man left, delirious with hypothermia and barely holding on to life, muttering over and over, "Poor boys, they are all gone."

As for the *Magruder*, if Kiah's crew were not able to save the foundering ship, at least their passage showed the best place for the leaking scow to cross the reef. Soon after the lifeboat's crew went under, the *Magruder*'s captain dumped his lumber cargo and piloted his limping ship down the same route that Kiah took across the reef. There were no casualties on the freighter.

While the men under Jerome Kiah's command went down as six more souls claimed by the Great Lakes, Kiah's near brush with death earned him a Gold Lifesaving Medal and an eventual promotion to district supervisor of the lights in the region. Yet though he lived a good number of years past that tragic April 23 morning, it seems that Kiah left a large part of himself with his ill-fated crew on the cold Huron waters that day.

Frederick Stonehouse tells the story of an eerie encounter near Saginaw Bay in his book *Haunted Lakes*. It was almost a century later—April 1965—and a man was taking his family for a recreational sailing trip north along Huron's Michigan coast. A thick fog had fallen around the ship late in the day, and though the sailor wasn't sure exactly where they were, the depth gauges indicated that the water below them was several hundred feet deep, so they were nowhere near land. He was just about to give his son the order to unfurl the genoa sail when impending disaster was suddenly staring him in the face. "This white rowboat boat just suddenly appeared dead ahead," the old sailor told Stonehouse. "I don't think it was 50 yards away! It was full of men…All were rowing, except for one standing in the stern who had his left arm and shoulder cradled over a long steering oar. He looked right at me and waved slowly with his right arm."

The man in the sailing boat bellowed a warning to his son and reamed on the helm, turning the ship hard astarboard. The boat lurched to the northeast, sending his boy sprawling onto the deck. He heard his wife, who was cooking dinner down below, yell out a series of curses as the pot of stew she was working on tumbled from the stove and onto the floor. Hunching low against the helm, he braced himself for the wood-splitting impact—but nothing came. When the man looked up to see if they had been able to dodge the oncoming vessel, all he saw was a thick gray fog all around his ship. While he acknowledged to Stonehouse that visibility was bad, there was no way that the ship could have disappeared so quickly…without even a sound from any of its crew.

His musings were interrupted by a sudden shout from his son. "Dad!" His son exclaimed, pointing down to the water, "I can see the bottom!" The man ran to the gunwale, and sure enough, he saw the top of a massive underwater reef looming just under the surface; the depth gauge read that there was a scant 5 feet under the ship's keel.

In a few more minutes, the water quickly dropped off again, and an hour later the fog lifted to reveal the Point aux Barques light shining to the west. It turned out that the man had underestimated the speed they were going, and the ship had made it to the mouth of Saginaw Bay much more quickly than he thought. As for the underwater ridge they had narrowly missed, that was the Point aux Barques reef, and it was then that it dawned on him how close he and his family had come to ruin on those rocks. Indeed, if it were not for that phantom boat that had suddenly appeared out of the mist and forced him to make the hard turn, he would have surely run the ship into the reef.

And what of that mysterious vessel? The man had considerable experience in the water, but had never seen such an old boat afloat. And where did it go after he had passed it? Not only did nothing happen when there should have been a fatal collision, but the fog was not nearly thick enough to allow the boat to disappear in a matter of seconds. The man telling Stonehouse the story was of a practical mind—not at all inclined to dwell on ideas of Flying Dutchmen. Stonehouse himself had talked to the man about his experience previously, during a time when he was just as skeptical about the supernatural. All that changed after a few years, when the author of *Haunted Lakes* became more receptive to the world of the paranormal. Recalling the old sailor's story, he did a little research on Point aux Barques.

It turned out that Kiah and the crew of the life-saving station went down right near where the sailor had seen the fully manned row boat, and that the physical description of the boat itself matched the make of vessel the 19th-century crew would use. It's hard to believe that a life-saving crew that went down in the line of duty over 100 years ago might still be patrolling the Point aux Barques reef. But that is the best explanation for the sudden appearance of an old rowboat that steered a man clear from a certain demise and then disappeared as silently and suddenly as it had come.

Seul Choix Point

Some paranormal experts have noted that cultures emerging from humid climates tend to have more ghostly legends in their folklore than cultures from arid regions. Time and again, it has been observed that areas near large bodies of water tend to be fraught with more supernatural activity than landlocked locations. For example, the damp locales of Scotland and Ireland have high incidences of ghostly activity. And what about the significant number of spectral tales told in monsoon India versus the sparse number of such stories that haunt the desert regions of Egypt? Does water truly beget ghosts?

Like everything else regarding the supernatural, the theory is riddled with uncertainty; surely there are plenty of other variables, such as population, history and culture, which may account for the greater number of ghosts in the damper regions of the earth. And then what do we make of the exceptions to these generalizations? The American Plains, for instance, are famous among paranormal aficionados for their high frequency of hauntings. Whether or not ghosts share a relationship with the earth's waters is up for speculation, but if one intends to argue that those beings of the netherworld are indeed aquatically inclined,

Seul Choix Point, jutting out from Michigan's Upper Peninsula, would be an excellent case in point.

The lone finger of land pointing down into Lake Michigan's northern waters is saturated with spirits. Stories of Indian graves, mysterious women gazing out the windows of empty houses, the sound of footsteps unaccountable to any material presence, wandering female phantoms and voices in empty rooms circulate around a cluster of old houses near the small town of Gulliver. The bizarre events culminate on the tip of the peninsula in Seul Choix Point Lighthouse—one of the most haunted lights that stand over the Great Lakes.

In the mid-18th century, Seul Choix Point was quite literally the "sole choice" for French voyageurs and Indians looking for a haven while ferrying their furry cargoes along the lake's exposed northern shores. As the fur trade ran its course, the erstwhile voyageurs' port became a thriving fishing center, and the peninsula turned to a bustling ground for a new, more settled, French-Canadian community. It seems that these first inhabitants established a strong attachment to their new home on the Upper Peninsula. For even today, long after time has claimed their corporeal essences, some part of these early settlers lingers over Seul Choix Point.

In a cluster of houses built next to an Indian graveyard, three homes seem to be a focus for paranormal activity on the peninsula. Frederick Stonehouse relates some of the bizarre events going on in these homes in *Haunted Lakes II: More Great Lakes Ghost Stories*. Stonehouse states that the ghost of an angry spirit, an Indian woman, lives in one of the houses.

Seul Choix Point Lighthouse is one of the most haunted lights that stand over the Great Lakes.

A broken clock hung in the kitchen of this home; the father noticed that the clock wasn't working one morning and told his son to throw it out in the swamp. Later that day, the boy threw out the busted contraption, and the matter would have been concluded right then and there —if the two lived in a normal house, that is.

Not two days had passed when the father, sitting with a neighbor at the kitchen table, noticed the clock hanging on the wall. He glared at his son, "I thought I told you to toss that thing out, boy." The child was genuinely amazed at the reappearance of the clock, and after a few moments of dumbfounded silence, protested his innocence so fervently that his father could only believe him. The neighbor did as well, and was spooked enough by the incident that he would never set foot in the house again.

On a cold winter's day some time later, another boy was walking home after hunting rabbits when he noticed a young girl staring out the second-floor window of that same house. Knowing full well that the place was supposed to be empty, he stopped and stared back for a few minutes when an icier, more profound kind of chill than the winter weather made its way up his back. Suddenly uneasy, he turned his back on the house and started making his way home. He looked over his shoulder after taking a few steps, but there was no one there any longer…the girl with the expressionless stare had just vanished.

There have been numerous other accounts of strange incidents in the house: of the wood stove acting up by itself even when unlit, sounds of footsteps upstairs when there was nobody there. The mysteries in the place developed another layer when renovations revealed secret chambers both in the attic and underneath the kitchen floor.

One of the house's previous owners had sealed shut a room in the attic; inside were a wealth of artifacts from the 1930s, including calendars, fishing equipment, old trunks and tins. The trapdoor concealed in the kitchen floor led to a hidden cellar that was much more eerie than the room upstairs. Apparently the room was intended as cold storage in the days before people had refrigerators; it was filled with cans of preserved fruits and fish.

But something much more difficult to come to terms with lay in the cold, dank blackness of the underground chamber. For there, partly imbedded in the sand floor of the sealed cellar, the homeowners discovered the skeleton of a young girl. When a worker was laying the foundation for a barn just outside, he dug up what looked like two tin coffin plates, one reading "Our Darling," the other engraved with "Our Loved One." Digging a little deeper, the man found what remained of a girl's shoe. With the Indian burial ground nearby, the skeleton in the cellar, and the coffin just outside the house, it is no wonder that there is so much spiritual activity taking place on Seul Choix Point. Strange voices and apparitions have been observed in the two surrounding houses. One day, several people spotted the apparition of a lone woman walking down the road from the beach; she drifted casually past the houses and disappeared into woods. Almost everyone there had recognized her from community photographs that were more than half a century old.

If Seul Choix Point might be able to compete for the dubious honor of most haunted place in Michigan, the peninsula's lighthouse is definitely one of the most talked of lights on the Great Lakes. As is often the case with Michigan's lighthouses, it seems that one of the light's long-deceased keepers still lingers in the station.

His name was Captain William Townshend, a British sea dog who immigrated to the United States in the late 1800s. In 1902, after working on the docks of Mackinac

Island for a few years, he was appointed keeper of Seul Choix Point. Given the lighthouse's uneventful history, his tenure as the light's keeper would probably have passed without notice if it weren't for the sudden illness that struck him early in August 1910. Townshend's brother nursed him as best as he was able, but the last two days of the keeper's life were spent in a bedroom at the top of the stairs, writhing in almost unbearable agony. He died on August 10 of that year.

History tells us that not much out of the ordinary transpired in Seul Choix Point when the lighthouse was still active. One of the Coast Guard's last keepers did report that fingerprints would mysteriously appear on the tower's Fresnel lens just after he had finished cleaning it. Perhaps Captain Townshend knew that the light's days as a manned station were coming to an end, and the old spirit was protesting the new era of automated lighthouses.

Accounts of strange occurrences began to circulate regularly after the light was automated in 1973. A caretaker was hired to look after the place when the Coast Guard abandoned it, and both he and his family were thoroughly frightened by more than a few inexplicable occurrences. The caretaker would later say that everyone in the family had seen shadows on the curtains of the upstairs windows when nobody was home. The sound of slow, leaden footsteps on the second floor would often wake everyone up in the middle of the night, and then there were those instances when a family member would be stricken by the overwhelming sense that something unseen was standing just over him or her, watching silently.

The frequency and intensity of these supernatural experiences increased after the Gulliver Historical Society bought the lighthouse in 1988. The first accounts came from inmates from the Camp Manistique Prison, prison laborers who were working on the first phase of restoration in the lighthouse. The fear in their voices made it clear that their complaints to the foreman weren't motivated solely by idleness. Stating flatly that they would do anything else that needed to get done in the building, several of the inmates refused to go the second floor, where they felt that same invisible presence that the caretaker had spoken about hovering just over them.

After that, the stories kept coming in. There was the carpenter contracted to do renovations who was frightened out of the empty lighthouse by an invisible person's footsteps. It was those same slow, plodding footfalls that started on the second floor but this time began making their way downstairs to where the man was working. He refused to work in the lighthouse by himself after that.

After the lighthouse was opened to the public, the most common report made by visitors was of a thick, sickly scent of cigar smoke that would suddenly waft over them on the second floor...when no one in the place was smoking. The dining room on the ground floor was also a hotbed of supernatural activity. Captain Townshend, not willing to let go of his English roots, was intent on having the dinner table set according to British custom. Day after day, the museum curator would come in to find the silverware rearranged to British style, with the forks turned tines down. Initially, the curator would take the trouble to rearrange the silverware, yet it was not long before it was decided that it wasn't worth arguing with the ghost, and the table arrangement was left alone.

Stonehouse tells the story of a television crew from a local station that came to the lighthouse in June 1997 to do a story on the building's restoration. One of the cameramen, intrigued by the pages of sheet music on the antique piano, put the music for one of his favorite tunes, "Spanish Eyes," on top of the piano's music holder. He and his crew left the lighthouse with the guides to shoot some footage of the grounds for a short while. Something inside the cameraman grew very cold when he returned to the room with the piano. There, on top of the sheet music holder, were the notes for "For Whom the Bell Tolls."

"Who rearranged the sheet music on the piano?" the startled man asked the guides. Not only could no one answer him, but they told the man that they would have been the last people in the room before they shot the footage of the grounds because the door had been kept locked during the tour. A few members of the television crew spent the night at the lighthouse; they were awakened several times in the evening by foul-smelling cigar smoke. The funk got so bad at one point that one of the crewmembers almost left the lighthouse for a motel.

As eerie as all these occurrences were, the most unsettling events involved the mirror in the upstairs bedroom. In the past, some people believed a mirror left uncovered in a dying man's room could steal his soul during the moment of death. People who have witnessed the ghostly mirror in Seul Choix Point may not be so quick to dismiss this belief as mere superstition. The large circular mirror rests in the same bedroom that Captain Townshend

*An isolated lighthouse is often
the last sight of drowning crews on the Great Lakes.*

passed away in; it is mounted atop a dresser and faces the
one bed in the room. On some nights, this mirror offers
much more than a reflection.

Witnesses have seen the placid glass surface suddenly
transform from a mirror to something like a window looking into another place. The reflection is replaced by thick
clouds of gray mist rolling violently just on the other side of
the glass. Before long, the swirling vapor begins to take
shape, gradually taking the image of a grinning skull. The

mist does not rest at this leering image, but continues to boil. Slowly, the head in the mirror forms distinguishing characteristics: a man, with bushy eyebrows, a long nose, and mustache and beard.

A woman who had recently moved to Gulliver with her husband glimpsed a much more concrete image of this man in the forest surrounding the lighthouse. "I was in the car with my husband, taking a ride for the day, and we decided to visit the Seul Choix Point Lighthouse," she tells Stonehouse in *Haunted Lakes II*. "My husband was driving and I was enjoying the scenery along Lake Michigan. As we approached the parking lot at the entrance to the lighthouse park, I looked over at a small clearing in the woods and noticed an old man leaning against a tree. He had a bushy white beard and eyebrows and was dressed in a dark blue uniform with matching hat."

The woman thought it odd that such a strangely dressed man would be just standing against a tree staring blankly into space. She blinked once, and he was gone. The woman told her husband what she had seen, but they both assumed that the man was one of the historical society's employees doing a re-enactment. A few months later, when she was reading a newspaper article her father had given her, the woman suddenly made sense of the figure in the woods. "When I read the story, I immediately got cold chills all over my body and I couldn't believe my eyes! It was a story about the ghost of Seul Choix Point! The man I had seen leaning against the tree and the man in the picture were the exact same!" For reasons she could never explain, she had been thinking about the lighthouse keeper in the woods since she had seen him. Now she knew why he had made such an impression—the man was a ghost.

So it is that the man in the mirror, the man in the woods, and the man in the newspaper are one and the same: Captain Willy Townshend, the old British seaman who manned the lighthouse from 1902 to 1910, smoked cheap cigars and died a painful death in the second-floor bedroom. Whether it is the circumstances of his death or the supernatural aura that seems to envelop Seul Choix Point that led to his haunting, the ghost of Willy is among the most active lighthouse phantoms on the Great Lakes. And to this day, visitors to the place are walking away with outlandish experiences. There have been sudden blasts of cold air in the light's halls; people who have tried to communicate directly with Willy have suddenly become violently ill; others have seen a dark figure walking across the hall in the parlor. And of course there's the overpowering cigar smell that wafts through the building, though no living person in the building or on the grounds would have the stomach to smoke such a smelly thing.

Stannard Rock

You could learn a lot about yourself working on the Stannard Rock Light. Some men were able to work in the lonely conditions for over 20 seasons without complaint, while for others, 6 weeks at the station was well past intolerable. Dubbed "the loneliest place in America" by the keepers who manned the station before it was automated, the lighthouse on Stannard Rock was built on a dangerous mile-long reef lurking just 4 feet below Lake Superior's surface. Located practically in the lake's center, the lighthouse juts out in the middle of a watery nowhere, a tiny manmade island built to warn approaching ships of the treacherous shoals surrounding the light.

For the men who worked the station, the 62-foot diameter crib was tight enough space as it was, but the psychological isolation of the surrounding water stretching out as far as the eye could see was often much harder to contend with. And then there are the accounts of mysterious forces acting in the region—of inexplicable magnetic disturbances, powerful enough to send ships' compasses spinning wildly, of almost inaudible voices that constantly whispered incoherent nothings to men who spent too much time in the area. Though the realities of the shipping industry in the Great Lakes necessitated a lighthouse on Stannard Rock, there was more than one strong indication that human beings did not belong there.

The treacherous reef was discovered by Captain Charles C. Stannard on August 26, 1835. A veritable underground mountain lying along one of the lake's major shipping routes, Stannard Rock was deemed a grave danger to navigation in

Lake Superior. Construction began on a lighthouse about 40 years later and was completed on July 4, 1882. Located 55 miles north of Marquette on the Upper Peninsula, the lighthouse at Stannard Rock lies in the heart of Lake Superior, and the keepers of the light would become first-hand witnesses of the lake's terrible magnificence. Manning the secluded light was soon recognized as one of the most difficult assignments on the Great Lakes.

It seems that there was little in the way of unusual occurrences for the first 60 years of the lighthouse's existence. Certainly, it was difficult, often terrifying work for the keepers. Situated in the angry eye of stormy Lake Superior, the lighthouse was open to the full force of the lake's rolling waters. It was often buffeted by waves over 100 feet tall, with the thundering waters cresting over the top of the tower's light. The lighthouse would shake to its foundations under such tremendous barrages, and we may imagine the effect it had on a keeper as cans flew from cupboards, chairs were hurled through rooms, and the very walls seemed to roar under the incredible strain. Yet the civilian keepers of the Lighthouse Service kept the light burning. Some of the men at Stannard Rock even seemed to enjoy the duty, one of them staying on at the lighthouse station for 20 years.

When the Coast Guard merged with the Lighthouse Service in 1939, the difficulties began. The rigid mindset of the Coast Guard did not seem to understand the nature of the prolonged periods of seclusion that were required on the station. Coast Guard officials changed the rotation schedule at the rock; whereas before, keepers spent three weeks at the light and one week off, the new rules stated that men were required to spend six weeks on and two weeks off. As well, the boats that the Lighthouse Service used to keep moored at Stannard Rock were removed by the Coast Guard, and whatever feelings of isolation the keepers struggled with before must have been intensified by a sense of being stranded.

What happened exactly to the first man who snapped at Stannard Rock is not known, but it would be a frightening testament to the power of loneliness if isolation alone were responsible. He was one of the first keepers assigned to the rock by the Coast Guard, left out in the middle of Lake Superior for six weeks with nothing but his own company. When a supply boat arrived about a month later, it was obvious the man had suffered severe psychological trauma. Gibbering incoherently about "the coming sea," he begged to be let off the rock. As shaken as the supply crew members were at the keeper's hysterics, they balked at leaving the lighthouse unmanned and tried to reason with the rattled man. They might have thought the keeper was bluffing when he threatened to swim ashore if he was not relieved immediately, but they knew he was serious when he made a sudden move for the edge of the lighthouse crib. Physically restraining the troubled man, the crew finally agreed to take him back ashore, away from the whatever demons tormented him at Stannard Rock.

The next keeper who went mad while working at the lighthouse was in much worse shape. A visiting relief crew found him lying on the crib under the open sky, soaked to the bone and shivering violently. He lay with his back to the cautiously approaching men, curled up into the fetal position, the sound of his unintelligible murmuring rising above the lapping water. Startled by the crew when they called out his name, the hapless light keeper leapt to his feet and came running at them with a bloodcurdling scream, punching, kicking and biting everything in his path. He was subdued only after the boatmen threw a straitjacket on him; it was then that they discovered what a month and a half alone had done to the man. His face, sunburnt and mutilated, was raked with dozens of long scratches stretching from his forehead to his chin. The men shuddered at the bloody tissue encrusted under his finger-nails, gruesome evidence that the keeper had taken to clawing his own face in his spare time. Apparently, he had a lot of it. The lone light keeper was never able to forget whatever horrors he endured during his six-week stay at Stannard Rock, spending the rest of his days tied up in a straitjacket in a Michigan asylum.

By 1961, the Coast Guard had come by a technological solution to the problem of manning Stannard Rock: an automated light. With all the necessary equipment being set up, it was to be the last year that members of the Coast Guard would have to fear placement in the isolated light-house. But on June 18 of that year, just before light keepers were to leave the station for good, Stannard Rock claimed its last victim.

It was almost 9:30 PM when a massive explosion erupted from the lighthouse's engine room, tearing up through the tower and incinerating everything inside it. There were four men stationed at the rock at the time. Three of them stumbled out of the burning structure—one badly burned man being supported by the other two. The only trace of the fourth was his key ring, found in the engine room where the explosion originated. It has been speculated that this man had caused the blast, sparking the fire when he walked into a dense fog of gas fumes in the engine room with a lit pipe.

While this certainly is a sound theory, this last mishap at the light only strengthened the foreboding aura around the place. The fiery tragedy that rocked the tower that June evening burned the mystery of Stannard Rock into the folklore of Michigan. Deserted ever since the explosion, the lighthouse still stands; the automated beacon still comes on at night, warning surrounding ships of the rocky danger just beneath the water. Yet more than the physical threat of the reef itself, seamen claim a dark, intangible presence warns ships away from the place. Coast Guard maintenance crews who routinely check the lighthouse have reported a strong feeling that they were not alone. There is a sense that something or someone still resides on Stannard Rock, staring out on the vast lake from the crib, pacing up and down the stairs of the gutted tower. So certain are coast guards of this presence that they refuse to inspect the lighthouse past dusk.

Perhaps it is the spirit of either of the two keepers who went mad on the rock, still trapped on the light long after they have passed on. Or maybe it is what's left of the one man killed in 1961—a bewildered ghost unable to come to terms with the instant and absolute eradication of its bodily form. Or then again, perhaps the presence is something else; something completely unrelated to anything human, dwelling over the vast underwater mountain of Stannard Rock; something that thrives in the heart of deep Lake Superior—something that wants to be left alone.

White River Light

Karen McDonnell, curator and resident of the White River Light Station Museum in Whitehall, Michigan, knows what it is to love one's work. She has spent almost two decades in the regal old lighthouse that overlooks the channel linking White Lake to Lake Michigan. Not that the picturesque brick and limestone building is a difficult place to love: over 100 years old, the antique sentinel on Michigan's west coast emanates the romance of a bygone age. Perhaps it is the dignified minimalism of the building's architecture, or the stalwart weight of the adjoining octagonal tower—topped by a watchful light that still comes on when the sun goes down. Inside, the waterborne relics from Michigan's past are exhibited in display cases. The obsolete sextants, beacon lights and compasses are impressive in their functional intricacy, testimony to the continuous inspiration humans have derived from the earth's waters...the same waters that can be heard crashing outside against the shoreline, a stone's throw from the lighthouse. For whatever reason, Karen feels more at home with every passing year that she spends in the White River lighthouse. And in this sense, she can relate to the spirits of the light's first residents who still seem reluctant to leave, although their bodies have been dead and gone for nearly a century.

Captain William Robinson was an English immigrant who arrived on the eastern shores of Lake Michigan sometime in the 1860s. A man who had been enamored with the water since he was born, he took it on himself to keep a beacon fire lit on the beach to mark the entrance into White

River for nearby mariners. Congress authorized a light-house be built for that purpose in 1866, and when the building was finally completed in 1876, the British captain was the natural selection as the lighthouse's first keeper.

He would end up spending the next 47 years of his life there—47 years in a building where he and his devoted wife, Sarah, joyfully raised 11 children; 47 years under the same roof that Sarah and two of his children died under; 47 years in a building where he eventually grew into a crotch-ety, stubborn senior. Through all of these episodes, the one thing that remained consistent was his duty to the White River lighthouse, the rigid routine that shaped a lighthouse keeper's days. Whether he had just held his firstborn in his arms, or it was the day after Sarah had passed away, Captain Robinson labored tirelessly at the lighthouse—year after year—until the building became an extension of the man himself.

It was 1915 when the government forced Robinson to retire because of his age. While he was able to arrange for his eldest grandson, William Bush, to succeed him as light keeper, the elderly man simply did not know how to live away from the lighthouse. Even after his grandson became the official keeper of the light, Robinson remained in the building and continued with the daily duties. When gov-ernment officials came by and informed the old man that only keepers' immediate families were allowed to board in lighthouses, the crusty old salt argued that his grandson still wasn't ready for all the responsibilities that a keeper took on. When it became clear that no exceptions—even for the wishes of a man who had put nearly half a century into his work—could be made to the regulations, Captain William Robinson fell into a deep depression.

The day for his departure drew nearer, and even when William Bush began packing his grandfather's belongings, the old man was still resolute. "This is my home, William," the stubborn ex-keeper said to his young grandson, "I'm not going to leave this light."

No one at the time could know how serious he was. Robinson was found dead in his bedchamber on the morning that he was supposed to leave. They buried him in the small cemetery on the other side of White River as he wished...so he could be as close to the lighthouse as possible.

The story makes perfect sense to Karen McDonnell. Not only is she able to relate to Captain Robinson's love of the place, a love that she shares, but the lighthouse's history explains the present-day activities in the old building. For Karen McDonnell is convinced that the captain and his wife are still in the White River Light.

The previous curator had warned her that there were spirits in the lighthouse, but the rationally minded McDonnell paid the man little mind. That was until about a month after she had finished doing her research on the light's first keeper. It was then that she began hearing sounds of footfalls upstairs on the second floor. The wooded floorboards would creak under someone's slow steps when the museum was well past closed and the lighthouse was definitely empty. Oddly enough, Karen was never scared of the presence upstairs. Certain that the halting steps belong to William Robinson, Karen confesses that she is somehow comforted by the captain's residence in the building.

In his seminal work, *Haunted Lakes: Great Lakes Ghost Stories, Superstitions and Sea Serpents*, Frederick Stonehouse quotes the lighthouse's curator: "The walking I hear is as if someone were checking. I have never felt fear, but as well, I have never gone to the upper stairs when I have heard it. I feel it is a ritual and that I shouldn't disturb it. It's calming."

McDonnell speculates that the captain is going through the same nightly ritual he performed during his many years as the light's keeper. After checking in on all of his sleeping children, he would walk up the spiral stairs to the top of the tower, inspecting the light one more time before calling it a night. Near the top of the tower one floor beneath the light, there is a window set deep into the tower's wall. Here William and Sarah would steal a moment from the hectic schedule of their day. Sarah would sit on the windowsill while William would recline on the stairs opposite her. They would talk about the day's work, the kids and anything else that came to mind, as the light of the setting sun streamed in through the tower window.

Robinson still rested here after his wife had passed away, silently enjoying his last pipe of the day while gazing out on the water of Lake Michigan. Many visitors to the lighthouse insist that they have experienced a strong pull to that spot in front of the tower window…that they have felt a quiet, calming aura on that staircase as they looked out onto the lake beyond. Karen McDonnell has attested that there is certainly something special about that one area on the spiral staircase.

Not only is William Robinson still doing his rounds upstairs, but Karen believes that he is conscious of, and quite pleased with, the work that she does in the lighthouse. She says that whenever she has finished a project for public display in the museum, the footsteps upstairs seem lighter, quicker, more energetic. Who knows whether old

Robinson enjoys the exhibitions himself or is happy about the fact that the history of his beloved lighthouse is being made available to all? Either way, McDonnell is convinced that he approves of the museum at the White River Light Station.

And then there is the ghost of William's wife, Sarah. Karen became aware of that ghost's presence after she placed a few old pictures of Sarah Robinson on display. It happened shortly after the diligent curator had put up a charcoal drawing of the tower's first matriarch. Ever since the picture went up, Sarah has been helping with some of the chores around the museum, where one display case on the second floor in particular regularly seems to dust itself. Karen has taken to casually calling out "Thanks, Sarah" whenever she discovers the dust rag sitting on the recently wiped glass case.

So it is that Karen McDonnell is now on a first-name basis with one of the denizens of the spirit world. Indeed, the fact that the White River Light Station is haunted has not bothered the curator in the least. Rather, she feels fine with the two spirits' benevolent presence, and likes the idea of an invisible watchman who still believes it is his responsibility to tend to White River's light.

The End

Collect the whole series!

America's colorful history is full of spine-tingling ghost tales
that will have you checking under the bed, behind closet doors
and in the basement. Haunting tales involve many well-known
theaters and buildings, many of which are still being used.
Stories range from the return of long-dead relatives, to phantom footsteps in unused attics, to whispers of disembodied
voices from behind the walls.

Ghost Stories of California	1-55105-237-7
Ghost Stories of Christmas	1-55105-334-9
Ghost Stories of Hollywood	1-55105-241-5
Ghost Stories of Illinois	1-55105-239-3
Ghost Stories of Texas	1-55105-330-6
Ghost Stories of the Rocky Mountains	1-55105-165-6
Ghost Stories of Washington	1-55105-260-1

$10.95 each

Coming soon...

Watch for these upcoming Ghost House Publishing books:

Haunted Theaters	1-894877-04-7
Ghost Stories of Indiana	1-894877-06-3
Campfire Ghost Stories	1-894877-02-0

Available at your local bookseller or from Lone Pine Publishing:
Phone 1-800-518-3541 **Fax** 1-800-548-1169